SURPRISED
by DOUBT

SURPRISED by DOUBT

HOW DISILLUSIONMENT CAN INVITE US INTO A DEEPER FAITH

Joshua D. Chatraw and Jack Carson

Brazos Press

a division of Baker Publishing Group
Grand Rapids, Michigan

© 2023 by Josh Chatraw and John Carson

Published by Brazos Press
a division of Baker Publishing Group
Grand Rapids, Michigan
www.brazospress.com

Printed in the United States of America

Library of Congress Cataloging-in-Publication Control Number: 2023002198

ISBN 978-1-58743-559-1 (cloth)

The characters in this book have been modified, but they are based on real people and interactions, trimmed and adjusted to fit this context. Some names and identifying details have been changed to protect the privacy of the individuals involved.

Baker Publishing Group publications use paper produced from sustainable forestry practices and post-consumer waste whenever possible.

23   24   25   26   27   28   29   7   6   5   4   3   2   1

To all the New City Fellows,
co-travelers who have joined me on pilgrimage—
limping, walking, and even sometimes
running together toward home.
—*Josh*

———————

For Erin.
Life with you is a true joy.
I love you dearly.
—*Jack*

CONTENTS

Contents

PREFACE

Confessions of a Theologian

SOMETIMES PEOPLE ASK ME if I (Josh) still have doubts. I sense that for many it's a surprise and a letdown when I tell them I do. Perhaps they like to imagine theologians, and especially apologists, as ironclad warriors who, having conquered all of their demons of doubt, are triumphantly parading with the angels from conference to conference, basking in the glory of victory. If that is your image of either of us, let me disabuse you of that notion from the start. The demons remain.

And they have left wounds. I can remember the anxiety I felt as a young college student when a professor exposed my ignorance of how the New Testament actually worked. I was a committed Christian but also a fairly naive business major taking my first religion class at a state university. My youth-group pizza parties had not prepared me for that.

In my twenties I felt the pain of being *that* guy in Bible studies— the one who couldn't get past the first verse because my head was spinning over whether this verse contradicted that verse, or what I was supposed to do with the Nephilim, or whether what I was learning about science could be squared with the opening verses of Genesis, or if . . .

Now, at least, the legions mostly hide out in the shadows. But doubt can unpredictably surface, gnawing at my faith with an intensity that rivals those earlier days. Another report of a school shooting taking the lives of children or a violent storm wiping out an entire village, and the internal rage erupts into doubt: "Why would a good God allow that?!" Walking through a museum, peering at the tangible traces of people who lived before Christ appeared in the world, I wonder, "Why did Jesus come so late?"

These questions are not new, and I know responses to them. I often go back to these responses after I get my emotions in check and also when I work through difficult questions with someone struggling with them for the first time. In the end, I'm not always sure which of the possible explanations is correct, but over time I've learned to accept unknowns. I've learned that maturity in life means living with different levels of confidence. I've learned to live with mystery. I like how the philosopher Christopher Watkin recently explained the paradox: "Christianity allows us to calibrate our knowledge of good and evil against something that is reasonable but that we do not fully know: namely God. So the world, for the Christian, is both more intelligible and more mysterious than for the rationalist: more intelligible because it does not rely on the skyhook of assuming ultimate rationality, and more mysterious because the character of the reasonable God is infinitely deep and rich."[1]

So, I live by faith in God, who makes sense of things. Still, there is so much *I* can't make sense of. As the apostle Paul puts it, I "see through a glass, darkly" (1 Cor. 13:12 KJV). Through Christ, I really do see. But the darkness lingers.

I say this not to valorize my own doubts but because the last thing you need is someone telling you faith is easy. At least for me, it hasn't been. The fact that you have picked up this book means that you're likely wondering whether you can hang on to your faith or whether you can return to the faith.

I believe you can—if you want to.

By this I don't mean that you can simply generate or sustain faith with a snap of your fingers. What I mean is that if you have a desire to believe, you can learn to seek in such a way that faith will be there in the end. That may sound fishy now, but give us a chance by reading the book through. And for now, hear this: Your doubts probably will not completely vanish anytime soon, but they don't have to have the final word. Doubt doesn't have to incapacitate your faith.

I believe in Jesus Christ and the claims of his earliest followers for a variety of what I find to be good reasons. I've learned to *keep* seeking, digging around in books, talking to other Christians, trying on ancient ways of seeing, and exploring new (but actually old) practices. In other words, through the years I've found ways to deal with doubt—not to vanquish all my doubts but to grow through, even with, them. I've learned God can mysteriously bring good from suffering, including the agony of my doubts.

Part of my job is to think hard about hard questions. Because I'm often thinking about these questions, it has occurred to me that I probably have had more doubts through the years than other believers I talk to in my community. I've had to constantly run things over in my mind. For over a decade I've had conversations about doubt with college students as a professor, and now I have these conversations in the fellows program I lead as well. One of the reasons Jack and I decided to write this book is that through the years we've had many conversations about doubt together, first when he was my student and then also as he became my colleague and friend. Reading this book will let you "listen in" on the kinds of conversations Jack and I have had over the years and, we hope, inspire you to build similar friendships.

In communicating with you by way of a book rather than in a conversation, we run the risk of not addressing the type of doubt or the kinds of objections that bother you the most. We can't reach through the binding, ask you questions, listen, be sensitive to how the Holy Spirit is working in your life, dialogue with you, and pray with you. The Christian faith is meant to be lived out with friends who will do all those things, which we can't do in a book. Nevertheless, because we've observed many people languishing in doubt all around us, we felt called to offer up this little book. In sharing what we've learned through the years, it traces at least one path to the faith, hope, and love we have continued to find in communion with a God who is really there, though who at times can feel hidden.

You might be interested to know that I only reluctantly took on the calling to be an apologist. In most of my theological circles at the time, the "cool" theologians and philosophers stayed out of apologetics. Peer pressure is no less powerful in the world of theology than it is on the playground, and I wanted to be part of the "in" crowd. Plus, I didn't care for heated arguments. At the time apologetics often felt to me like what college freshmen did late at night in the dorms, one upping the other with abstract arguments that most people couldn't care less about. But I sensed the Lord calling me into it, so I went, albeit aware of the dangers.

The Oxford scholar and apologist C. S. Lewis, whose spirit will accompany us through this book, once closed a lecture to a group of apologists like this:

> I have found that nothing is more dangerous to one's own faith than the work of an apologist. No doctrine of that faith seems to me so spectral, so unreal as the one that I have just successfully defended in a public debate. For a moment, you see, it has seemed to rest on oneself: as a result when you go away from the debate, it seems no stronger than that weak pillar.[2]

Lewis understood what it was like to know an argument like the back of your hand and *win* with it. But he also understood what it was like to still be haunted by lingering questions: What if I've missed something? Am I just playing intellectual games? Does this doctrine really mean anything to me? Does it matter? It is one thing to argue a point, another to live it out, especially when disillusionment and suffering unexpectedly disrupt your life.

We academic types often hide our wounds behind our intellect. One of the side effects can be a failure to humbly open ourselves up to the God we believe our arguments point to. Consider that God might be using your doubts to make you vulnerable so that you can learn to receive his presence as a gift—rather than something you imagine you can control or earn. Much of my life—my work, my sense of worth, my identity—has operated from the slippery logic of achievement. I now see how that burden seeped into my faith. Painfully, I've had to learn the hard way what I always confessed I believed: I can't earn the grace I need. And it has been in the quiet waiting on the Lord—amid my doubts—that I've learned to receive it.

Lewis warns against reducing Christianity to an intellectual exercise in which God is the end of the logical chain of syllogisms by which the really smart people become Christians. This is not how Christianity works. Lewis would go on to say that those of us who set out to defend the faith, and I would add anyone who is attempting to work out their faith intellectually, "take our lives in our hands and can be saved only by falling back continually from the web of our own arguments, as from our intellectual counters, into the reality—from Christian apologetics into Christ Himself."[3] We should work things out in our minds as best we can, but our best arguments are meant to point us to Jesus Christ. Our arguments can only gesture to the deeper reality to which we must humbly open ourselves up by experience and practice.

This book doesn't attempt to tidily answer all your questions; that would be glib. Nor do we think that we will make all your doubts disappear; that would be naive. While we hopefully will answer some of your questions, more importantly, in what follows you will find ways of thinking differently, practices to engage in, and better questions to attend to—with the aim of trying on what Lewis described as the reality of Christ.

Two final notes are worth mentioning before we get started in earnest. First, we will sometimes use the word "deconversion." As you likely know, Christians have long debated whether someone can genuinely be converted and then "fall away." We both have our opinions about that topic, but we don't take a position here. Instead, we simply use words like "deconversion" to describe the phenomenon of someone no longer confessing Christ. We don't mean anything more than that, and our conversation doesn't hinge on whatever side of that theological debate you fall on.

Second, we've tried our best to keep this book practical and fairly short. Most of the time, people do not need an academic tome.

Throughout, Jack and I interact with and summarize scholarly works, look back at history to gain perspective, and refuse to shy away from hard things. Yet we have prioritized concision and clarity. We know this will leave some of you wanting more, so we've left a paper trail of resources for further reading in our endnotes. We've taken this approach because we want you to finish the book you're holding in your hands. But we also think it is a mistake to suggest, tacitly or otherwise, that you can simply think (or read) your way out of doubt. Better thinking is part of it, but better thinking calls for better vision and better posture. Herein we aren't just offering you ideas to think about. We're offering you a different way to "comport yourself towards the world,"[4] which might just lead you to a deeper faith, even amid your doubts.

> Jesus said to him, "If you are able!—All things can be done for the one who believes." Immediately the father of the child cried out, "I believe; help my unbelief!" (Mark 9:23–24 NRSV)

Josh Chatraw
Summer 2022
Raleigh, North Carolina

Part One

THE ATTIC

1

This Isn't How They Told Us It Would Be

IT SEEMED EASY TO BELIEVE IN CHRISTIANITY when I (Jack) was surrounded by friends who were all devoted believers. My youth-group years taught me to believe that Christianity was transparently true; doubt was portrayed as an embarrassing and possibly deadly disease. So, if we had doubts, we kept them to ourselves. None of us wanted to be seen as a project.

Of course, we knew people who weren't Christians and had heard some of their objections, but these were hardly to be taken seriously. We were told that these objections had been answered, and we were reassured that Christianity was right and they were wrong. Anyone who was willing to look at the evidence could see as much. After high school I enrolled in a Christian college and joined another community that reinforced this kind of never-doubting belief. It all seemed to "work" just fine.

Until it didn't.

Little did I know that those years—filled with worldview retreats, purity pledges, and jeremiads about "*the* culture"—were setting me up for some serious disappointments. Faith isn't nearly as easy as

I thought. And as it turns out, I'm not the only one who learned this the hard way.

When I was in high school, Jim was one of the most active members of my youth group. He attended every gathering and was friendly with everyone. Wise, honest, and full of conviction, Jim was the perfect picture of a faithful Christian young man. We lost contact with each other after high school, but I recently reconnected with him through Instagram and learned that he no longer considers himself a Christian. He had, apparently, first experienced doubts while attending our youth group. As far as I know, he never told anyone. Perhaps he was worried about the social stigma; maybe he was tired of hearing the all-too-familiar arguments as if they were enough.[1]

When he went off to college, Jim's seedling doubts grew into something he couldn't ignore. He began identifying as bisexual. In the church environment we grew up in, there wasn't much of a positive sexual vision on offer. Instead, we were taught rules and a certain sensibility: being gay was simply wrong and gross. Little more was said about it. I guess it isn't very surprising that Jim isn't a Christian after more than eight years in that environment. Christianity didn't seem to fit Jim anymore.

Ashley was, like Jim, a professing Christian. She grew up attending a private Christian school, and her entire childhood was steeped in a particular brand of Christianity. Her parents kept her from dating, bought her a purity ring, and sent her off to a Christian college to—presumably—find a nice Christian husband. They didn't quite get the outcome they hoped for.

As Ashley began to reflect on her childhood, one word began to dominate her memory of it: abusive. Not abusive in a physical or sexual sense but abusive in relation to her intellectual and emotional freedom. Her beliefs had been forced on her, and her freedom of thought had been restricted. At first, she thought her parents were an anomaly, and she explored other forms of Christianity. Yet the succession of Christian authors she encountered only frustrated her faith. Each of them seemed so confident, and they all wanted her to believe exactly what they believed. They were like her parents. Ashley wanted to be a Christian, but the whole structure of the religion felt tainted. The whole thing just seemed to be about power. This feeling was exacerbated as she began to see spiritual leaders—the same ones who had taught her to "keep herself pure"—rally their congregants around proudly immoral politicians. I've pleaded with Ashley that Christianity is broader and richer than the specific kind of parochial Christianity she grew up with. I've tried to show her that the failures of particular leaders don't demonstrate the failure of Christianity itself. But for Ashley, Christianity just doesn't seem good anymore.

Taylor, like the others, came from a Christian home and grew up in a conservative environment. She had been voicing doubts for a long time before she arrived at college, and it seemed to her that no one had satisfying answers. Taylor was particularly concerned with how Christianity and modern science related; she wanted to know how Christianity explained the data that led so many people to accept evolutionary theory. The desire to answer these questions and solve her doubts was so strong that Taylor pursued a minor in apologetics.

Taylor's search seemed to work—at first. She would find a satisfying answer to some issue—say, criticism of the New Testament's historical reliability—and would be certain of the Christian faith for a while. Eventually, however, a new argument challenging Christianity would present itself in some YouTube video or Reddit thread. The new argument would throw Taylor into another season of doubt, and the cycle would continue. Eventually, Taylor lost the motivation to remain a Christian. It was too much work; there were too many arguments against Christianity. At least for now, Taylor has given up on trying to banish the doubts that have plagued her for so long. She has deconverted.

As I have watched these friends and others struggle with their faith, I have become convinced that I was misled. Don't misunderstand me: I still believe Christianity is true. But neither Josh nor I believe what we were once told growing up—that the Christian faith will always appear obviously true to anyone who looks at the evidence carefully.

The Christian faith isn't always so easy.

So, let's get this out of the way right here at the start: If you are no longer sure if you can believe in God, or if you're beginning to doubt Christianity, we don't assume you've lost your mind. We assume you've thought things out, and we respect your willingness to grapple with doubts and the problems within the community you've grown up in. Grappling honestly with these doubts often leads to "deconstruction"—a prolonged process of examining and replacing previously assumed belief structures. While deconstruction sometimes leads to deconversion, it doesn't have to.

You Aren't Alone

One of the most challenging parts of deconstruction is the overwhelming loneliness that accompanies it. Deconstruction, to some extent, sets you apart from the community you've lived in, and figuring out where to turn or whom to talk to can be a lonely process. Perhaps you are reading this and still consider yourself a Christian but the community you once held dear wouldn't consider you "in" anymore. Or maybe you have left the church behind and you now feel the absence of belonging. Many people have a hard time replacing the deep bonds and the sense of meaning the Christian community once gave them.

Deconstruction can drive loneliness in more than one way. In many cases, at the core of deconstruction lies a distrust for established authority structures and norms, and this distrust often leads to angst and cynicism. How do you know whom to trust? Are people just trying to manipulate you into conforming to their beliefs? What is the line between getting to know someone, with all their hopes and beliefs, and letting someone's faith journey—an inherently emotional topic—have ill-suited sway over your life? Building relationships becomes hard when you feel that people are trying to win you to their side. The loneliness only deepens.

The truth, however, is that deconstruction today is a well-trodden path. People have experienced your doubts before, and many will likely experience those doubts after you. Sometimes these doubts

lead people away from Christianity; other times people find themselves drawn deeper into the faith, more steeled and humbled than
before. Both steeled *and* humbled? It's a strange and wonderful
combination that will come into focus in part 3 of this book. For
now, the point is simply that you aren't alone in wrestling with your
doubts—no matter what dogmatic "Why would you ever think that?"
remarks you are hearing.

New Pressures

Over the past five hundred years, the Western world has seen massive upheavals in how people perceive the world around them.
Where humans once would have turned to family and an inherited community to define themselves, that responsibility now rests
largely on the individual's shoulders. We still gather in communities
to make meaning and understand the world, but now we *choose*
our community, our beliefs, and our identity. Every group we're
connected to asks us about religious beliefs, social stances, and
political views. *You* must pick a side. And your family or tradition,
it is assumed, should not shape that opinion; you have to do it on
your own. This is one of today's great sources of loneliness and
angst. It is up to you to figure it out. If you have a soul, it is up to
you to save it. This is a crushing burden to bear.

Adding to the pressure of figuring out the mysteries of life un-
tethered from a community with deep inherited bonds of trust,
a vast amount of raw information is now available to help you
choose. Whereas humans once did not feel the pressure of religious
views outside the ones they inherited, we now find innumerable
competing views at our fingertips. What we have, then, is a two-
edged sword: you are called upon to be the master of your own
beliefs—without the help of established communities—yet the path
to mastering your beliefs runs up a growing mountain of data and
argumentation.

This isn't all bad; questioning the beliefs that have been given
to you is an important part of growing up. We've learned from the
past that simply trusting what is handed to us can lead to disastrous

consequences. The teachings of different traditions often conflict. We need a way forward that appreciates the wisdom of different traditions without blindly going along with error. Access to more data can be helpful, but we also need access to sources of wisdom that help us sort it all out. The absence of such sources results in pressures that can feel crushing.

The modern tornado of information and competing views, hurling internet articles and YouTube videos every which way, has led to fear-induced responses. Some communities have attempted to build a space where people can comfortably shelter in place, hidden away from the crosswinds of competing options. Many believers who walk through deconstruction were born into one of these protective communities. Their childhood faith community feels uneasy, situated in a world of radical individualism and limitless information. As a result, these communities build walls to keep out the dangerous voices and ideas.

The defensive walls become pervasive. They seem natural and even go unnoticed. Until one day—like Jim, Ashley, and Taylor—you not only notice the walls but also long to get past them to the world outside the shelter. So, you lower your shoulder and plow right through. To your surprise the walls you always thought to be sturdy and thick are paper-thin. And instead of finding level ground on the other side, you fall hard and fast from a second-story attic. It's to this collision that we turn in the chapters ahead.

2

An Invitation to Explore
the House of Faith

BEFORE HE WAS A HOUSEHOLD NAME, C. S. Lewis was a hardened atheist. From his teens to his early thirties, he vocalized many of the objections to Christianity that animate doubt in our age.

After his surprising conversion Lewis famously portrayed Christianity as a house with many rooms. He invited people through the front door of the house and into the hallway of faith rather than into a specific room. His aim was to offer a "mere Christianity"—by which he meant an account that included the core elements of the faith and didn't get into intra-Christian debates and differences—as a way into the house of faith.[1] This invitation was framed for those who had never been Christians. For those of us who grew up in Christian households, our experience is slightly different from that of Lewis's primary audience, but the house analogy is still useful when we reflect on our modern situation.

Lewis's house of faith has many rooms, with each representing a certain way of being Christian. These rooms represent unique combinations of denominations, cultures, and eras. All the rooms are united by a shared belief in Jesus Christ, articulated by the

9

ancient creeds of Christianity and what the early church called the "rule of faith." This analogy rests on a specific claim: there is a unity amid diversity. The multiple rooms within the house represent the many ways communities have embodied the faith.

The Attic

The problem is that some strands of Christianity do not recognize themselves as simply one room within a larger house. They give the impression that their room (and maybe a select few other rooms) is the entire house. This claim of exclusive legitimacy is not always explicitly stated, but the tone, posture, and messaging of leaders leaves little doubt as to their opinion of the other rooms. The result is that the questions of faith are framed in a particularly narrow way.

Does this sound all too familiar? If so, you may have long been inhabiting what we call "attic Christianity." If you grew up in the attic of the Christian faith, questioning the walls of your room can feel like questioning the entire house. Built in fear to protect you from the dangers of the world outside, the attic demands a loyalty that makes the slightest deviation feel like heresy.

The attic you're likely familiar with, however, is a somewhat recent addition that stands out from the rest of the house but feels normal if you grew up in it. Why wouldn't it feel normal? It might be the only room you've ever been in. To top that off, an entire subculture of Christianity speaks as if life in the attic is simply the way faith must work. Author Abigail Favale illustrates this in her deconstruction story. Favale, now a Christian and a professor at the University of Notre Dame, recalls being "raised in a corner of Christianity that was more or less ahistorical, one that viewed our local church as a seamless extension of the earliest Christians in the New Testament. I was not even self-consciously Protestant, unaware that Evangelicalism is itself a tradition, the newest kid on a longstanding block."[2] Favale explains how this lack of awareness led to some real problems: "I naively assumed that my familiarity with Scripture made me an expert on Christianity writ large, and I wasted no time in hastily constructing a flimsy scarecrow version of it, one I could easily tear down."[3]

Perhaps you, like Favale, have grown disillusioned with attic Christianity. What once felt safe now feels confining. You realize the air has long been rife with either an ahistorical anti-intellectualism or a quasi-rationalism operating from a severe inferiority complex: there is little room to explore new scientific discoveries, ideas from outside the room are met with suspicion, and you're experiencing a malaise due to years of inhaling the fear and angst that fills this attic.

Who exactly is in the attic? Fundamentalists? Well, yes. But the term "fundamentalist" is often used haphazardly, merely as an insult that confirms one's group identity over another. However, if a community self-describes as "fundamentalist," it is a pretty safe bet they're in the attic.

How about those who describe themselves as evangelicals? Here things get a little more complicated. Some communities that identify as evangelical are certainly inhabiting the attic. The key for American evangelicals is to be able, as historian Mark Noll puts it, to realize that "what is *distinctive* about American evangelicalism is not *essential* to Christianity."[4] If a community is unable to distinguish between the two, in theory or in practice, it likely resides in the attic.

While we've both considered giving up on the label "evangelical" because of its political and cultural baggage, we still consider ourselves evangelicals, albeit a certain kind that has left the attic. We're like "wounded lovers," as Noll put it, still married to the broader, global evangelical movement.[5] Lewis, on the other hand, was not an evangelical. (And two guides who will come to our aid later—Augustine and Pascal—were long dead before evangelicals came onto the scene.) But don't miss the key point: by "attic Christianity" we mean an instinctually narrow way to inhabit Christianity, a fundamental posture that confuses a Christian group's *distinctives* for Christianity's *essentials*.

So, then, why build the attic? There will be more on this question later. But for now, it bears mentioning that at least one of the reasons an attic has been erected is due to fear—the desire for the "safety" of being far away from the world outside the home. Attic builders want extra barriers and firmer standards so they can attain certainty and be free from contamination or doubt. They don't want to lose what is most important to them or have the next generation walk away from faith. They want the comfort and the security of having arrived. Most of us can at least understand these motivations.

Unfortunately, attic dwellers often resort to making caricatures of those outside the attic. And while building strawmen is easy to do in the attic, dismissing people with different views as simply deceived by the devil or unwilling to "look at the evidence" is a bad long-term plan for keeping curious, empathic, and hurting people in the house.

Furthermore, the attic builders too often decenter the attic from the historic essentials shared by the other rooms and set up their theological distinctives as load-bearing walls. The remodel, as it turns out, makes for rather cramped quarters. If you have been stooped over in this confined space for too long, a misaligned posture has likely set in. Rather than rallying around the historically defined essentials of Christianity and celebrating the beauty and joy of the good news Jesus first presented to the world—what Lewis meant by a mere Christianity—attic dwellers build defensive walls to keep the people inside safe and the wrong people out. Too often, these insular walls built for safety are not shaped by the ancient structure and beauty of the rest of the house; they are built in reaction to modern pressures. When the world outside the house acts, attic Christianity reacts.

These reactions often result in frantically built structures designed for immediate safety. The problem, however, is that these walls might not actually be protecting your faith. In fact, they could be suffocating it—especially if it is a faith that is seeking understanding in a highly pressurized world of competing options. In contrast with the newly discovered world outside a childhood community, the insulated culture of the attic begins to feel small. Attic Christianity seems to be hiding something from you. Life is not nearly as simple as the leaders in the attic cast it to be. And once someone stumbles upon troubling questions, forcing them into a closet is a surefire way to grow doubt into something unwieldy.

Brian Zahnd explains this problem with metaphors that are at home in our attic:

> By mispresenting the Enlightenment and the corresponding rise of empiricism as an existential threat to the Christian faith, many frightened Christians sequestered themselves in panic rooms of certitude. But this kind of darkness breeds monsters. Most doubt—like monsters—are not that scary in the daylight. Most Christians can deal with inevitable doubts as long as there is room for doubt. But when a system is enforced that leaves no room for doubt, benign uncertainties can mutate into faith-destroying monsters. When doubts are locked away in a closet of secrecy, they can grow into formidable ogres.[6]

If you grew up in the attic and have begun to feel the walls closing in—or, to use Zahnd's language, you find yourself running from monsters—the trust that once gave you confidence in the attic now gains a haunted edge. Was your trust misplaced? Were you tricked? The arguments that once seemed like knock-down evidence for Christianity begin to feel like they could at best go either way. To make matters more concerning, the hypocritical behavior of so many Christian leaders and the instrumental use of faith for the ends of power and control further undercuts confidence in the attic's trusted guides.

In this book you will not find any pleading for you to remain in the attic if you are still there. In fact, we don't advise you to stay. The good news is that jumping out of the window—out of Christianity altogether—isn't the only way to leave the attic behind. There are better ways to exit.

The Main Floor

Although the view of the landscape outside the window might be appealing, jumping isn't the best option. And if you are going to leave the house of faith, why not just walk downstairs and have a look around before you walk out the front door? Why not explore the foundation of the house? You may be surprised by what is essential to the house and by the wisdom and beauty offered by those who have been living beneath your feet all this time.

The floor below was built long ago, with capacious rooms and sturdy foundations. There is space to grow, enchanted beauty to discover, mysterious corners to explore, and ancient wisdom etched in the stone pillars. Plus, a view from the main floor allows for a closer inspection of the grounds outside the house; perhaps, after you look around the main floor, the leap of doubt won't be as alluring. Walking downstairs allows you to begin reimagining life in the house of faith, and this will mean more than taking a new intellectual perspective. It will also call for a new way to attend to the world.

At this point you might be thinking, Yes, I have experienced the problems of attic Christianity, but I have also already explored the whole house and rejected the entire structure! If so, we would ask you to consider that the attic might have had a bigger impact on you than you realize. As we will see in the following two chapters, if you grew up in the attic, it has shaped not only *what* you believe; it has shaped *how* you go about trying to believe. Unlike the attic, the main floor has space for wonder and awe. Absolute certainty isn't a requirement. Questions are encouraged. Answers are meant not to shut down mystery but rather to open up new ways of seeing and better questions to ask. Inhabiting the main floor doesn't just offer a better perspective; it corrects one's posture. It teaches us to walk differently.

At least it did for us. Once we walked downstairs we met some characters who have helped us stay in the house. We've learned from stories that span over two thousand years—stories from Augustine to Blaise Pascal to C. S. Lewis (each of these will serve as a tour guide of the main floor of the house) and many others—we've learned that we are not alone. They, too, had doubts and fears, but they, too, encountered a mysterious grace in the wounds and words of Jesus.

Learning to attend to all of life as an undeserved gift, as Christianity teaches, kindles awe and opens up intellectual vistas, expanding one's vision of the world while also offering the wisdom needed not just to cope but to find peace in the midst of pain, uncertainty, and failure. This means you must learn to embrace mystery and learn to wonder. Yet this is a far cry from anti-intellectualism. Our guides will offer us a different rationality from the narrow rationalistic certainty that many grasp for today. They have helped us see how Christianity offers a deeper and more capacious rationality.

Of course, even if you take us up on this invitation, you might explore the main floor of the house and still decide to leave. And there's always the chance that we're wrong. Maybe the magnetic Jesus we encounter in the pages of the Gospels can't be trusted. It could be that Christianity is nothing but wish fulfillment, nothing more than an illusory product of evolution that so many people have embraced only in order to help them survive and pass down their genes. But then again, atheism could be its own wish fulfillment. And to paraphrase the philosopher Alvin Plantinga, if we could be wrong about Jesus, we also could be right.[7] We can't escape taking such risks when it comes to the big questions of life.

Even if you may end up leaving, our advice is this: Don't take a leap of doubt. It's a long way down from the attic. At least explore the house first, and if you still decide to leave, walk out the front door.

3

Looking Back to Look
at the Attic

IF YOU GREW UP IN ATTIC CHRISTIANITY, it has shaped
the way you see and weigh the claims of Christianity. In chapter 6
we'll see an example of how attics of some sort aren't altogether
new; they've been constructed at different times and for different
reasons. Our main focus is on the attic as a room that exists today
within the Christian house. This attic has been built as a reaction
to fairly recent cultural changes and is, in some important ways,
different from the rooms on the main floor. But in order to get a
wider view and gain some perspective on our modern-day attic,
we will now briefly look at three historical periods of the house of
faith. This historical perspective can help us, for it is easy to wrongly
imagine our situation and the pressures that accompany it as being
either universally common or utterly unique. By spending the next
few pages looking at aerial pictures of the Christian house, we will
place ourselves in a better position to move forward wisely.

Period 1: The House of Faith Is Formed

It's the first and second centuries, and Christianity has recently
arrived on the scene. At this time, it is widely seen as a new sect of

Judaism, and Christians are a fringe group with little to no political power. Becoming a Christian provides no social advancement. For many, it is a strange and audacious religion that sees "in a twisted and defeated corpse the glory of the creator of the universe."[1] Since pretty much everyone at this time believes in a spiritually charged world, the miraculous claims of Christianity aren't the problem. What *is* audacious, however, is the claim that God stepped into the world to die and rise again as an act of love. The people of this time, just like people today, knew that the dead don't come back to live eternally. Yet something strange was happening: there was a small but growing number of people who were buying it. In the decades that followed, groups of Christians continued to grow, despite facing periodic schisms and persecutions. Even so, these first few centuries were filled with competing worldviews, and it would be several centuries before Christianity would become the default option. This means most people didn't simply inherit Christianity as the commonsense perspective. The contestability of these ancient Christians' faith provides seekers today—especially those trying to leave the attic—with helpful guidance that is worth exploring.

Period 2: The House of Faith Has Grown

During the Middle Ages, roughly AD 500 to 1500, we see that Christianity, once a strange and fringe religion, has become the default worldview for those in the West. The contestability of belief that the early church faced is gone. Christian practices and ideas are now embedded within cultural habits and social institutions. As the central religion of the Western world, Christianity now has enormous social power and influence; it's the air people breathe. If you were to ask someone of this time and place, "Do you believe in Christianity?" the answer would be some version of "Well, of course."

Similar to the ancient world, people during the Middle Ages still assume a spiritually charged world, but with an almost exclusively Christian bent. Demons, angels, and the Holy Spirit are considered part of the fabric of everyday life and are assumed to be mysteriously at work behind the scenes. As the philosopher Charles Taylor puts it, during this time, "atheism comes close to being inconceivable. . . . It just seems obvious that God is there, acting in the cosmos, founding and sustaining societies, acting as a bulwark against evil."[2] For most people of this period, Christianity is the only game in town. Some people fall out of favor and face excommunication, but even those people rarely question God altogether.

Period 3: A Divided House of Faith and an Emerging Disenchantment

In the sixteenth through eighteenth centuries, we begin to see some shifts that make faith in God feel more fraught. By the time we reach the modern world, these shifts would make God seem unnecessary and implausible for some. First were the rising pressures of contestability. In 1517 Martin Luther hammered out his *Ninety-Five Theses*, his actions serving as a historical marker for what will become known as the Protestant Reformation. As the Reformation progressed, people increasingly had to choose a side: "Which Christianity should I believe in?" In time, people felt more of a responsibility to choose what to believe; each believer became their own "priest." It eventually was no longer realistic to simply receive the belief of one's community. Each person had to choose which community of faith to join. The weight of belief began to fall on individuals. This didn't lead to widespread doubt about Christianity itself—at least not at first. The struggle for some early on was in determining *what kind* of Christian to be. But eventually, with the emergence of new technologies that gave the average person access to more diverse options, this contestability grew deeper and more widespread.[3]

Second, the Reformation was one factor among many that contributed to "disenchantment"—the collective loss of the sense that the world is charged with sacred meaning and spiritual activity. Much scholarly ink has been spilled in arguing how large a role the Reformation had in creating a world where people don't assume the existence of a spiritually charged cosmos. If you read Martin Luther and John Calvin, you'll see that they were unshakable in their belief that the world was God's theater and that the devil and his minions were actively at work. The first Reformers were not critiquing the idea of an enchanted world but rather what they believed to be un-biblical superstitions infecting the Roman Catholic Church at that time. Subsequent Protestants went further, however, and opened the door to disenchantment wider.

Third, people began to imagine the universe according to new metaphors—a shift toward viewing the cosmos as mechanical or watch-like. Whereas people had once imagined the cosmos as a living organism or harmonious orchestra, subscribers to the new way of thinking preferred the metaphor of a machine. With dis-enchantment, people were less inclined to assume a spiritual re-ality infusing the world. Instead, they settled on the idea of two distinct—and increasingly separate—domains, one "natural" and the other "supernatural." Yes, most still believed God existed, but gradually his supernatural realm was disconnected from the natu-ral world. Instead of spiritual realities being constantly at work in every aspect of creation, they became detached forces with little bearing on the machine-like natural world. Some concluded that the supernatural was not necessary at all. The growth of disenchant-ment was not solely the result of a budding mechanistic view of the universe, but the idea of a machine-like cosmos dovetailed with other developments, and soon traditional Christian beliefs began to feel less plausible.[4]

Early Deconstruction

These social, theological, and philosophical shifts combined to produce atmospheric changes. New pressures on Christian be-lief were in the air. Some cultural elites were beginning to doubt Christianity. The Protestant Reformation had disrupted the long-standing authority structures of medieval Europe, and there were now multiple competing claims to sacred authority, all calling themselves "Christian" while denying the Christian status of other groups. This caused some people to begin challenging sacred authority altogether. And some saw the religious wars and the sheer number of diverging philosophies as reasons to doubt those religious claims to certainty.

Amid this whirlwind of change and uncertainty, it is not surprising that some began looking for ways to cope. The sixteenth-century French philosopher Michel de Montaigne is one such figure, and he serves as an early exemplar of what many describe today as "deconstruction." For Montaigne, the human condition is unavoidably immanent. Trying to discover and master sacred truth, as the Protestants and Catholics claim to do, is hopeless. Instead, Montaigne argued that everyone should embrace the mystery of life and seek to be happy in simple, everyday joys. Montaigne saw religion as a byproduct of geographical location and time, and as such it was not something worth arguing about. Who knows what's right? It is best, then, to pursue a happy life in the present without connection to a larger sacred order. In some ways Montaigne, while remaining formally Catholic, embodied deconstruction long before the twenty-first century.

Contestability led Montaigne to doubt the possibility of rationally justifying any answer to the transcendent questions of life. Though Montaigne was only one early-modern figure promoting this skeptical approach, his ideas proved influential. His proposed solution was something like, "Live life as it comes at you, and don't become overly passionate about anything." Or in more philosophical language, one should pursue "immanent contentment."[5]

An Early Attempt at Reconstruction

How would people respond to this early form of deconstruction? Here we turn to another representative figure, the philosopher René Descartes.

Descartes did not like the open embrace of mystery and uncertainty that Montaigne had endorsed. As Sarah Bakewell says, Montaigne's brand of skepticism frightened Descartes, driving him to innovate:

Descartes's real innovation was the strength of his desire for certainty. Also new was his general spirit of extremism. Trying to get way
from Skepticism, he stretched it to a hitherto unimaginable length,
as one might pull a strand of gum stuck to one's shoe. There could be
no question of floating in doubt indefinitely, as on a "sea of specula-
tion." Uncertainty was not a way of life, as it was for Montaigne. . . .
For Descartes, it was a crisis stage.[6]

Descartes, however, believed he could quell the crisis. His solution was to isolate himself in a room with his thoughts and doubt
the existence of everything. Through this process he found the one
thing he could not deny: his own existence! After that, he carefully
built an argument by which he could conclude with certainty that
God existed. "Certainty for Descartes," as Michael Allen Gillespie
explains, "arises when we can no longer doubt, that means at the
end of the path to doubt."[7] This inward turn, this attempt to isolate himself from contingent factors and eliminate anything that
could not be proven autonomously, was a different path from that
previously taken by thinkers in the Christian tradition. Many later
embraced this posture, or something like it, in the hopes of casting
off contestability and doubt.

This new posture contributed to the Enlightenment, a movement
that, despite developing differently in various contexts, emphasized
reason as the ultimate authority and, in some places, questioned
the legitimacy of sacred authority. As far as we are concerned,
Descartes's desire to remove contestability backfired: as people
embraced his posture, many of them grew wholly unsatisfied with
his proofs for God. An approach that encouraged the removal of any
belief that could be doubted ended up leaving many people riddled
with doubts. This approach along with the modern world's disenchantment, helped open the door to deism, a belief in a distant God
who operates within the bounds of what can be proven according to
Enlightenment rationality. And this eventually exposed the public
to what not long ago felt unimaginable to most: the possibility of
not believing in God at all.

Looking Forward to the Attic

In a later chapter we will return to Descartes and Montaigne to contrast their postures with that of another philosopher, Blaise Pascal. But for our purposes, zooming out to this broader history of doubt, contestability, and disenchantment provides some historical perspective on contemporary experiences within the attic.

Montaigne was disillusioned with anything fervently religious and was skeptical toward certainty given the plurality of opinions about life. In response to doubt he charted out a way to "lay hold of the present goods and settle ourselves into them."[8] In promoting a worldly path to contentment, he became a forerunner of what has become one of the dominant spirits of our age. And in many ways the attic itself is an attempt to protect Christians from the demons of contestability and worldliness that haunt the modern world. Today we are surrounded by a cacophony of competing voices that is far beyond anything Montaigne experienced. He possessed the education and leisure time—both rarities in his day—to feel the cross-pressures of competing philosophies and ask, "What do I know?"[9] Today we need only step outside our front door, or scroll through Twitter feeds, or turn on the television to feel the push and pull of contestability and find ourselves asking the same question.

Builders of the attic have, at times, reacted by using Cartesian claims of certainty to ward off Montaignian cynicism. They tout their own use of reason and have a tendency to cast their conclusions as common sense while implying that those who see things differently are morally or intellectually inferior. They reassure their followers that attic Christianity has all the answers. Even thirty years ago, before the internet made the world, and the attic, feel smaller, some people inside the attic detected overreach. Today, in a world full of online windows into other spaces, more people who grew up in the attic are starting to sense that such grandiose claims are little more than spin.

And then there is Montaigne's pursuit of contentment through a self-focused worldliness. His pursuit has reached new heights in a consumeristic and affluent West. Leaders of the attic have perceived a growing moral laxity and decadence and have reacted by working to maintain safe places free from worldly contamination. To be fair, we agree that our contemporary world is trapped in reductive moral visions. Skepticism is not conducive to human flourishing; discovering purpose and meaning in life beyond ourselves is needed in order to sustain the human spirit and generate thriving communities. And yet, caught up in what has been cast as a war against *the* culture, attic Christianity has too often allowed anger to cast a shadow over the intellectual and moral vices rampant in their own room. As we will see in the next chapter, fear has driven leaders in the attic to hastily add on protective barriers that can inflict more damage than they prevent.

Further, attic Christianity hasn't done well in helping the disillusioned and intellectually curious sustain faith in an age of contestability and disenchantment. Ironically, by largely responding to these developments in a modernistic posture, it has often shielded its occupants from some of the treasures found on the main floor of Christianity. We will get to those treasures soon enough, but next we need to walk through the attic to see how growing up hunched over under low ceilings might still be affecting the way you approach the entire house.

4

Life in the Attic

IF YOU'VE MADE IT THIS FAR IN THE BOOK, chances are you or someone you know keeps bumping into the rafters and the walls of the attic. Or perhaps you have already taken flight. This chapter attempts to articulate some of the attic's unique pressures. Of course, no two experiences are alike. Humans and social movements are complex. Our tendency to make either saviors or devils out of individuals and groups often hinders us from seeing the truth clearly. Our goal in this chapter is not to give you rocks to throw but to share some common experiences so that you might better understand your own past and move forward with wisdom.

The Pressures of the Attic

In his landmark work *The Scandal of the Evangelical Mind*, Mark Noll recounts how the evangelical movement, in reaction to modern developments within culture, has often been marked by in-group splits and a distrust of intellectual pursuits.[1] These sectarian and anti-intellectual attitudes have made for tight quarters in the attic. But before we explain further, recall that both of us consider ourselves "evangelicals" in some sense, as does Noll. We are *not* implying that all evangelicals reside in the attic; however, Noll's analysis suggests a pattern we should pay close attention to.

If you've ever been under a low, slanted ceiling, you know that the rafters often force you to stoop over as you walk around. This isn't a big deal if you are making a quick trip to the attic to grab those old high school yearbooks. But imagine trying to live up there. Years of hunching over would leave you with misaligned posture. Likewise, attic Christianity conditions you to stoop over. You've learned to live with it, so this bend in your back and the crick in your neck can come to feel like the normal Christian way. Yet, constantly bending over puts pressure on your joints, so you can't help but sense that something isn't right.

Rafter 1: Make Up Your Own Mind . . .

The attic has been built with a fierce commitment to individual choice in matters of faith. Some have even said that this commitment to individual autonomy is a feature of Protestantism.[2] In our view this idea requires nuance. It is better to say that what began as a rightful rejection of corrupt clericalism and the denial of direct access to the Scriptures for the common person eventually morphed into radical individualism. In any case, let's take a closer look at how individualism affects attic Christianity.

Taking responsibility for your beliefs is a healthy part of growing up. Blind faith leads to disappointments and pitfalls. But attic Christianity has taken the supremacy of private judgment to an unhealthy extreme. In the attic, individualism has nearly eradicated expertise. If private judgment becomes the sole and final judge of belief—if you alone must weigh the truth and reliability of any claim—then assertions of "expertise" begin to seem manipulative.

Adding to the unease is an extreme biblicism in which each person is solely responsible for reading the Bible and deciding what is true, why it matters, and how they should live. Historically, Christians have relied upon the ancient creeds and church traditions in mapping out the core elements of the faith. The early Protestants, while not necessarily *bound* to tradition, saw the collective wisdom of the church as a guidepost that was confirmed by fellow travelers who had already explored the crossroads of faith. Attic Christianity has undermined these sources of support. While some in the attic may still nod at these ancient ways, in practice their identities are formed more by their stances against contemporary Christian rivals than by the doctrines and practices that have long bound Christians together.

With this low-hanging rafter in mind, we want to introduce you to Daniel. Born into a Christian family, Daniel began to explore his faith seriously as a teenager. His parents had taught him about Christianity since he was young, and part of their teaching was that each person should read Scripture to discover truth for themselves. Like many young people in these communities, Daniel was drawn to eschatology, the doctrine of the last days. As he read the Bible, however, he came to an understanding that was very different from that of his parents. Hunching under rafter 1, Daniel thought he would be fine making up his own mind. But then he bumped into the next beam hanging over his head.

Rafter 2: . . . In the Right Way . . .

While attic Christianity trains you to decide for yourself what to believe, its leaders expect everyone to choose the "right" beliefs. Even though the supremacy of private conscience is fiercely defended in the attic, little space is allowed for differing beliefs. "Think for yourself" is what is said, but then communicated in a thousand little ways is the more important addendum: "as long as you are thinking like me."[3]

Leaders in the attic have too often assumed, as Noll puts it, a "lack of self-consciousness characteristic of the nineteenth century's confidence in science."[4] While the nineteenth century was full of incredible scientific discovery, it was marked by hubris about its methods. A similar hubris fills the attic air. Leaders in the attic often assume there is one straightforward solution to most theological questions. They mine the biblical data and then proclaim the answers. Since they view their process of discovery as being objective, they consider their solutions to be perfectly evident to all honest and sane people.

This shift to an increasingly quasi-scientific approach to theological questions has minimized three things that historically have been prominent in Christian thought.

First, if each question can generate a sure and obvious answer, mystery is minimized as a vital part of Christian thought. If there is something about God or the world we want to know, we can figure it out.

Second, if each person can attain these clear and obvious answers on their own, then humility in our conclusions seems irrelevant. The logic looks something like this: The "commonsense" reading of the Bible (i.e., the way everyone in my particular community reads it) clearly teaches the earth is six thousand years old, or that women shouldn't work outside the home, or—in the case of Daniel—when and how Jesus is coming back. To suggest otherwise is not simply to be wrong but to put the structure of the entire house in jeopardy. For if you aren't subscribing to, say, the "natural" reading of Genesis 1–2 and rejecting everything but a strictly "literal" interpretation of the entire passage, then what stops you from denying the literal resurrection of Jesus?

Third, if someone rejects the clear and obvious answer that you have found, generosity is no longer an ideal that constrains you. Anyone disagreeing with the obvious answer is ill informed, ill intended, or one step away from destroying the entire foundation.

What does this all mean practically? For Daniel, it meant that his newfound opinions on eschatology, a complex topic long debated, became a source of tension and anxiety. His new beliefs greatly concerned his parents. They worried that their son was being led astray. Eschatology led to an existential crisis.

Rafter 3: . . . On Every Question

Daniel's exploration of eschatology marked the beginning of a long road of anxious doubt. He kept exploring the faith that he was born into, and he kept asking questions. It might have been livable for Daniel to force himself to hold the "right" beliefs on a few theological questions. After all, even the main floor of the house requires adherence to some "right" beliefs and ways of living. The Trinity, the deity of Christ, and the bodily resurrection of Christ have always been essential Christian beliefs. The attic's third rafter, however, expands the realm of core beliefs far beyond the historic boundaries.

The third rafter of the attic pressures people to treat more and more questions as tests of orthodoxy. After all, if you accept that a clear and obvious answer can always be found in the Bible, and you further believe that Scripture speaks to all areas of life, then every question in life should have a clear and obvious biblical answer. If you deny that answer, so goes the logic, you must be denying the Bible's sufficiency or authority.

Therefore, you feel as if, in order to be a faithful Christian, you must have the right view on everything from vaccines to Harry Potter, science to beer, national politics to yoga. And the right view is the one that lines up with the attic's leaders. And so we hear leaders proclaiming things like, "The Christian worldview gives you only one option on who to vote for as president!" Leaders who say such things do not necessarily believe those who vote differently aren't Christians. Even so, such pronouncements form communities beholden to a slippery-slope mentality that is always on guard for any hint of deviation from the safe path. After all, what a leader speaks about most frequently, passionately, and directly will be what their followers assume is most important. If a leader seems to tilt every conversation toward court rulings and primaries, why wouldn't his listeners assume such topics are matters of orthodoxy?

For Daniel, this meant that the life of the mind became a mountain to climb with a frightening abyss at every turn. Daniel wanted to own his faith, and he had been told that he should make up his own mind. But as he did this, he felt extreme pressure from the people around him to align his thoughts with theirs. Worse yet, if his thoughts veered too far, his standing within the community was called into question. If he switched some of his political views, or shifted his views on gender roles within the church, or changed his views on baptism, his community would question his Christian faith. Encouraged to make his own decisions yet subverted in his attempts to think independently, Daniel found that cognitive dissonance was his constant companion.

Daniel's story is not unique. For so many in the attic with similar experiences, the heart of the New Testament's vision of the Christian life—faith, hope, and love—is gradually overshadowed by fear, anxiety, and disillusionment. As these pressures are mixed with broader secular challenges of contestability and disenchantment, sustaining one's Christian commitment becomes extremely difficult.

The Walls of the Attic: . . . While Remaining Pure

And then there is sex.

The entire house has always been concerned with morality, but attic Christianity has a habit of weaponizing it to guard against "the culture." Remember, the attic was formed in part to protect people from the world. One of the best ways to do this, by the logic of attic Christianity, is to establish walls that keep young people away from a degenerate moral landscape. Continuing from the certainty and self-assurance that comes from rafters 1 and 2, rafter 3 pushes leaders of the attic to establish an ever-increasing number of new walls to provide safety from the world.

One of the most obvious examples of this in recent memory is the purity movement of the late 1990s and early 2000s. The Christian house, reflecting on God's good creational design, has long held that sex is to take place between a man and woman in marriage. Leaders within the attic responded to Western societies' growing acceptance of nonmarital sex by establishing guardrails. If dating leads to premarital sex, the logic went, then young people should simply not date. Instead, they should take purity pledges and focus on platonic friendships with the same sex. The walls were a sort of shield that would eliminate the risk of premarital sex, the heartbreaks associated with dating, and the growing rates of divorce. For example, I (Josh) was admonished and ostracized in my second year of college by other Christians for taking a classmate out on a date—alone! They explained I was "practicing for divorce" and "playing with fire."

The purity movement has since received widespread criticism for the way it shaped young people to think about themselves, grace, and Christianity as a whole. These problems should not be used to discount the clarity of the Bible's call for a sexual ethic that is currently countercultural in the West.[5] Yet, in some communities, extrabiblical "purity talk" took center stage and pushed other biblical concerns to the background. The dangers of hating outsiders and the ease with which we can lack charity for our neighbors, for example, didn't receive nearly the same attention as did violations of purity codes, dress standards, and modes of courtship. In such cases attic Christianity buried the good news of forgiveness and grace beneath a mound of extrabiblical badges of righteousness that promoted fear and shame.

The purity movement is one example of how extra barriers built into the attic shape the way inhabitants attend to the faith. Leaders in the attic establish strict protective walls around all sorts of things, from entertainment to education. This leads to the creation of "negative reference groups," which "serve in [attic dwellers'] minds as models for what they do not believe, what they do not want to become, and how they do not want to act."[6] Depending on the section of the attic you grew up in, atheists, "the woke," and liberals may be "negative reference groups" you've encountered. In such cases the attic's restrictive boundaries develop an "identity [that] depends on a logic of 'us-against-them.'"[7] In other words, an individual's core identity is decentered from Christ and is re-centered on what or who she is *against*. Conversations about grace, forgiveness, love, and hope become rare. When they are mentioned, they produce little energy or affection. Instead, feeling embattled, the human heart races to dwell on how ghastly *those* people are. "God, I thank you that I am not like other people—robbers, evildoers, adulterers—or even like this tax collector" (Luke 18:11).

Even as you are reading this, you are at risk of rooting your identity over and against the attic. "God, I thank you that I am not like people who still live in the attic." That isn't the way to flourish. It's the path to a life of bitterness and anger. In Luke 18, Jesus offers a path to true thankfulness and joy through humility before God.

There's another issue with *how* walls are built in the attic. Since leaders create these barriers in response to changing cultural pressures, they are—by necessity—shifting. As the perceived threats to Christianity change, so, too, do the measurements of purity within the attic. For example, the idea that due to moral-purity concerns young people shouldn't date one another has fallen out of popularity. During the COVID pandemic, however, some portions of the attic saw the rejection of masks or vaccines as an essential test of Christian faithfulness. This constant changing of the walls follows from the nature of the attic as a shelter from the world. The attic community has taken up a "rhetoric of resentment"[8] that reinforces the practice of defining itself in opposition to others. For obvious reasons these shifting standards make growing up in the attic stressful, particularly when its members are trying to "make up their own mind" about more and more issues.

Worse, the negative reference groups used to shore up one's Christian identity can become more confusing and less effective as one ages. Once you actually meet "them," you discover that people outside the church are often thoughtful and caring. So, you wonder why your church taught you to view them as malevolent enemies. And as revelations of improprieties—from cynical power games to ruthless toxic behavior—inside the attic stack up, disillusionment sets in. You wonder, What has this all been about?

Where Do You Go from Here?

If you grew up in the attic, you might naturally attend to Christianity and the world in some of the ways we've described in this chapter. It's important to note, however, that attic Christianity mixes historic Christian truths with the rafters and walls we've discussed. Attic Christianity claims that Christianity entails a certain way to live and think. It also says that Christianity's teaching on life and morality goes with the grain of the universe. Attic Christianity is correct about both of those general points. But the irony is that while prioritizing its critiques of surface-level changes in culture, the architecture of the attic can leave you trying to make up your mind about Christianity with a misaligned posture.

If you, like Daniel, have viewed the faith as solely an intellectual system that will answer all your intellectual curiosities, what happens when that system leaves some questions unanswered? What happens, for instance, when you realize that Christianity doesn't neatly *solve* the problem of evil? Or what happens when the fight against culture becomes the rallying point for churches while the scandalous grace found in Jesus is glossed over? Or what happens if you follow a list of purity do's and don'ts but your marriage still falls apart? What happens when the trickle of scandalous revelations becomes a flood of stories that point to gross negligence and abuse committed by prominent Christian leaders? Christianity begins to seem like a part of the problem rather than a solution.

None of these observations are meant to undermine the foundation of the Christian house. But we do mean to subvert the attic's reductionistic frame. The problem is not that attic Christianity calls for purity and sound doctrine. The New Testament does the same. But attic Christianity has isolated, expanded, and improperly framed these teachings. The center of Jesus's moral vision is focused on the inner workings of the heart and an inward posture that leads to human flourishing in a broken world (Matt. 5–7).[9] The New Testament is less a book of rules for every situation and more a compass that directs our lives to our true north. This new direction, and the obedience that comes with it, is grounded in forgiveness and love rather than fear and guilt. Rather than simply being books of case law to plug and play into our contemporary world, books full of propositional data mainly to be mined and formulated into abstract doctrines, the Scriptures offer us stories, poems, proverbs, and letters that invite us to live with transformed visions and hearts. As the theologian Kevin Vanhoozer puts it, "Scripture summons the intellect to accept its propositions, but it also summons the imagination to *see*, *feel*, and *taste* them as well."[10]

Attic Christianity hasn't done enough to counter the disenchanted and intellectual assumptions of our modern world. In response to the contestability of our modern age, leaders in the attic have often claimed it can produce evidence that demands a Christian verdict. It has too often responded to doubt by reducing

Christianity to a system of data. Do you doubt? Just look harder at the evidence. Or the opposite advice is given: "Just believe." But if you continue to have doubts, what does that imply? That you are unable to follow the logic? That you are emotionally compromised? That you are somehow defective for not being able to "just believe"? Such thinking obscures the give-and-take relationship between our doubts and our beliefs, both of which are rooted in far more than a simple chain of arguments.

As we saw in our last chapter, our culture has shifted in ways that have affected Christianity's plausibility. The assumption that spiritual realities are active in the world is no longer woven into the fabric of society. Quite the opposite. In our modern Montaignian world, our daily patterns lead us to sense that the most real and important parts of our lives are the material goods in front of us. In such a society, God can seem less necessary, less real. At their deepest levels belief and doubt are not driven *simply* by logic; what we believe in, find plausible, and doubt is ingrained into us by the assumptions we've inherited and imbibed from cultural habits, symbols, and narratives. To explore our doubt and faith wisely, we shouldn't naively rush head-first into syllogistic arguments or lines of evidence. Though there is an important place for such reasoning, we need to first examine our posture.

And to get our bearings we must learn to keep the main things the main things, leading to a cleared-eyed view of authentic Christianity. The Christian faith has a storied tradition of critical inquiry and nuance, but its best thinkers have emphasized that the faith is impoverished when reduced to an abstract philosophical system. Christian faith is a response to an encounter with the living God in the person of Jesus Christ and the mysterious work of the Spirit. The main floor is built upon a claim about an event: God entered space and time in the person of Jesus to save a broken and rebellious world. To explore these truths as the essence of Christianity—the *rightful* walls—you will need to leave the attic, suppress the urge to leap from the window, and walk downstairs. Bringing your doubts and beliefs to level ground is the best way to determine whether to leave through the front door or make your home on the main floor.

5

Finding a Better Posture

WE ARE NOW READY to step into how you might answer *the* question.

Does God exist?

Some people believe they can *prove* he does. They may take you through the classic proofs of God's existence or dive headlong into scientific arguments. After all, what started all this? Something must have. God did. Case closed. Still others are quite convinced that they can *prove* God doesn't exist; after all, how can an all-loving, all-knowing, and all-powerful God allow evil? Where is God when children are tortured? Or where was he when millions of people were exterminated in the Holocaust? Checkmate, theists. Not so fast, says the apologist—and the debates continue, round after round. You've probably seen this before. Argument after argument is made by smart-sounding people. If the standard is absolute proof—for or against God—it's understandable that a typical observer would be tempted to give up on the God question altogether.

We're oversimplifying a bit here. Unbelief and belief now take many forms. Technological progress and increased mobility have made interacting with new viewpoints a daily occurrence. In our pluralistic age the God question can be dizzying. It's also disorienting to try to constantly dismiss the beliefs of your friends, coworkers, and classmates as ridiculous when you know them to be reasonable people. But if you take them and their various convictions seriously, as we should, then eventually an emotional-social vertigo can set in.

Western society has moved from having a single, almost unquestionable majority view to having a plurality of viewpoints, both religious and irreligious. As prefigured by Montaigne, this shift has left many people fragile and insecure about questions of faith.[1] This is where you might be. You've peeked through the window of the attic and seen secular people who are not immoral, dumb caricatures. In fact, they are often quite smart and kind. So, you ask, "Now what?" The more you have explored, the more you have felt the pressures from the opposite sides of the God question. Who really knows? "Maybe," you've begun to think to yourself, "the best thing would be to give up on answering the question and stay as neutral as possible, living life as it comes."

But here's the thing: While you might have given up on "proofs," giving up on answering the God question is something you cannot do. You inevitably answer the God question every day. Life will come your way, and how you navigate it will relate to what you believe or don't believe about God. The God question is not going away. So, as we think about how to answer this question, we want to introduce you to four common postures that people assume, often unconsciously.

Posture 1: Clench Your Teeth, React, and Ridicule

Those who take this posture assume there is nothing to learn from alternative positions, which are intolerable, even evil, and must be driven from public view. This posture reduces people to caricatures, and those who have the "wrong" beliefs are the enemy.

In this way attic Christians and headline-grabbing New Atheists can have a surprisingly similar posture. On the latter side a small group of loud voices claims that belief in God is not only irrational but also dangerous. As one popular book argues, religious belief "poisons everything."[2] On the other side those shouting from the attic sometimes claim—echoing the famed Enlightenment thinker John Locke—that "promises, covenants, and oaths, which are the bonds of human society, can have no hold upon an atheist."[3]

When the two camps debate ultimate concerns, the debates are filled with what the philosopher Charles Taylor calls "conversation-stoppers"—which sound like, "I have a three-line argument which shows that your position is absurd or impossible or totally immoral."[4] This flexing doesn't lead to wisdom, for it short-circuits learning and undermines conversations that have the potential to bring insight.[5]

Posture 2: Lean Over, Focus Narrowly, and Achieve "Certainty"

While some Christians in the attic embrace a kind of anti-intellectualism, others pursue a quasi-intellectualism that justifies Christianity with what they imagine is something like raw intellect. They respond to the God question by building from the floor up, reasoning with one plank of truth at a time until they've completed a unified structure made entirely of logic. Reason, they think, is the neutral arbitrator for determining truth about life, God, and ultimate reality.

This approach might seem like something for smart people, but most philosophers today consider it a dead end. Sure, there are some truths of basic logic or math recognized as being universal. But when it comes to life's big questions, there is no universal, agreed-upon system of reasoning. In fact, the overarching systems of rationality are themselves contested. As the philosopher Alasdair MacIntyre has stressed, when we are speaking about the big worldview questions of justice or practical rationality, we must ask, "Whose justice and which rationality are we talking about?"[6] Even if someone does not realize it, they are making "rational" judgments in light of a framework that they have in some sense trusted by faith. It cannot be proven by empirical or logical evidence.

If we are hoping to use basic logic and raw data to solve the God question and reach an answer everyone will agree with, we will be disappointed. Consider how we choose our spouse, or our vocation, or who or what to make sacrifices for. We don't just two-plus-two our way to life's most important decisions. If "reasoning" about the question of God is reduced to logic chopping or data processing—both of which have their places in answering life's smaller questions—the result can be a malformed Christian faith. The Bible becomes a storehouse of data, with the disciple working as a logician who syllogizes conclusions or as a lab tech who searches for reproducible data. But this is the wrong posture. Once you've adopted it, you have, perhaps unwittingly, closed yourself off from seeing the bigger picture and attending well to the question of God.

Posture 3: Shut Your Eyes to Give Up (but Not Really)

Postures 1 and 2 can eventually lead to a loss of hope in answering the God question. Apathy sets in, and the existential questions related to the God question (Who are we? Why are we here? What happens when we die?) are impossible to answer with confidence. In response, you might be tempted to be "free" and float through life, avoiding taking any particular stance.

But trying to float through life leads to a *functional* view of life in which we act out whatever view is most prevalent in our particular time and culture. If you were previously trapped in the attic, then leaving so you can "live life as it comes" only leads to a new residence—with its own walls. There is no place to live that is free from constructs. As C. S. Lewis puts it, "You can step outside one experience only by stepping inside another."[7]

While we aren't able to solve the question of God in the way posture 2 suggests, we can't ignore the question either. Reality pushes back on us. People close to us die, and we can't help but ponder what awaits them. We make judgments. We label actions as being good and evil. We assign value to things, people, feelings, and experiences throughout every moment of each day. And we can't seem to shake the feeling that certain things in life are sacred. We all have to cope with the question of God as we interact with questions of meaning, significance, and morality by way of our decisions. If you choose to give up, you aren't really giving up; you're accepting the answers of the socially constructed space you happen to live within.

Giving up is still wagering.

Posture 4: Stand Up Straight to Look At, Look Through, and Step Into

Though we never left Christianity, we both have gone through intense periods of doubt. For a time, I (Jack) would flip through every apologetics book I could get my hands on. I googled obscure arguments and skimmed Reddit threads. Keeping with the posture I had learned in the attic—posture 2—I kept looking for a silver-bullet argument that would banish my doubts once and for all.

Sometimes my faith was bolstered by the logical deductions and historical arguments I learned from my apologetics classes. But as I grew older, I started feeling unsatisfied. No argument was airtight. There was always a gap in the evidence or a path to escape the Christian conclusion. The Reddit threads were full of commenters who found the arguments wholly unsatisfying—and had long lists of reasons why Christianity was wrong, absurd, or even immoral. Their cynicism fueled my doubt. It also deepened my desire to find an apologetic guru with evidence demanding an unassailable verdict. This furious searching, coupled with the rising fear that it would never end, filled me with existential dread.

For those of us who grew up in a church that demanded certainty, doubt can itself become quasi-evidence against belief. The dogmatic voices of former church leaders still echo in my head: "Are you a hundred percent certain? If not, you are a hundred percent lost." If you struggle with doubt, that's scary as hell. If certainty is attainable, why can't I find it? What's wrong with me?

However, the root cause of this disappointment and dread is *not* the insufficiency of the arguments; it's the standard for belief. Evidence and careful reasoning are important, but arguments alone can't provide definitive proof or banish doubts entirely. But if we can't find the answer to life's most important questions by breaking down arguments into their smallest components or by executing a string of Google searches, how do we move forward?

For both of us, the key was learning a posture suggested long ago by C. S. Lewis. In his short essay "Meditation in a Toolshed," Lewis gives us a metaphor that will guide the posture we are inviting you to try:

> I was standing today in the dark toolshed. The sun was shining outside and through the crack at the top of the door there came a sunbeam. From where I stood that beam of light, with the specks of dust floating in it, was the most striking thing in the place. Everything else was almost pitch-black. I was seeing the beam, not seeing things by it.
>
> Then I moved, so that the beam fell on my eyes. Instantly the whole previous picture vanished. I saw no toolshed, and (above all) no beam. Instead I saw, framed in the irregular cranny at the top of the door, green leaves moving on the branches of a tree outside and beyond that, 90 odd million miles away, the sun. Looking along the beam, and looking at the beam are very different experiences.[8]

When looking at a beam of light, we can see some remarkable things, like the floating particles within it. But when we look *along* (or through) the beam, we can see the world illuminated.

Lewis is arguing that if you aren't willing to look at the beam *and* along the beam, your vision of the world will be distorted. The anger and fear inside the attic discourages this open posture since it can feel risky. Yet to develop the humility needed to live a good life and answer the God question with wisdom, we must learn to stand up straight and look both *along* and *at* everything.

In the pages ahead we will model a way to cope with life's complexity and diversity. As contingent creatures thrown into this world with a history behind us and limitations we cannot escape, we always have more questions than answers. Accepting that mysteries will always remain and that we can't escape into nowhere to solve the question of God, we will compare and weigh competing options by looking *at* and *through* the perspective of some of the most influential residences for those jumping out of the attic. Then we will do the same kind of evaluation for the main floor of Christianity.

As we look at life's biggest questions—What are we doing here? How should we live? What happens after we die? What if God is real? What if God doesn't exist?—we will inquire about how different residences respond. In comparing the different structures, we will explore which best accounts for the human experience, best accommodates what can be observed, is most structurally coherent, and can be inhabited most consistently.

We all have to live somewhere. The wisest way to go about searching for our true home is to keep in mind our full humanity—which includes our intellectual, emotional, and imaginative faculties—and look for a fit.[9] Finally, stretching Lewis's metaphor, in our final two chapters we will suggest ways you might wager on Christianity by *stepping into* certain ways of living within the Christian house, yet this time surrounded by ancient architecture.

Part Two

OUTSIDE
THE HOUSE

6

New Atheism

WE WOULD LIKE TO INTRODUCE YOU to someone who jumped from an ancient attic of sorts hundreds of years before our modern version was built. As it turns out, this ancient doubter became one of the most significant voices to ever reside in the house. Augustine of Hippo's life story reminds us that even revered saints were sometimes critics of their childhood faith.

Augustine was a prodigious young man who was raised in the backwaters of the Roman Empire. Think small-town fundamentalist church in the Roman Bible Belt. For young Augustine, Christianity was basically synonymous with authoritarian leaders, hard-and-fast rules, and literalist interpretations of nearly everything. While Augustine's father was a pagan, his mother was a Christian. Monica was devout, loved her son, and wept for his salvation. As a Christian helicopter mom—to use a modern term—she tried just about everything to keep him in the church. But for an ambitious, curious, and intellectually gifted teenager like Augustine, the walls of his fourth-century attic were never going to hold.

When Augustine was young, Christianity was a major force in the empire but had yet to become the default cultural position. People had options and felt pressure to choose between different religious claims. Augustine writes of this pressure in his spiritual autobiography, *Confessions*, when he tells of leaving Christianity to try to find coherence and truth in other options.

As a young man, Augustine chased achievement and status. He worked hard to be someone important and got himself into centers of power and influence—but he couldn't escape a nagging sense of guilt and a deeper hunger. He explored a dogmatic rationalism through a religious sect called Manichaeism. The Manichees claimed reason apart from faith. They straightforwardly proved truth, so they thought, and ridiculed Christians for relying on faith. Augustine ate up this macho rationalism—for a while. He came to see that the Manichees mocked religious believers while touting unproven assumptions that had to be taken by faith. Such a duplicitous approach led to self-contradicting dead ends. As we will see in this chapter, the builders of the attic are not the only ones prone to overreach.

For a brief time Augustine tried to be a kind of skeptic. But he came to realize that he needed something more. The ancient skeptics were right to critique the overreach and arrogance of dogmatists, but in Augustine's eyes they didn't offer a real way forward. Plus, Augustine was haunted by Christ. During his journey away from the stifling walls of his childhood version of the faith and then back to the Christian house, Augustine developed the right *posture*. He learned to lift his eyes to see beyond the attic. He suffered his way to a humility that produced a deeper way to know.

Augustine was also changed by the lessons he learned while exploring options outside the Christian house. He did not dismiss all that he learned during his time of wandering; he found truths outside the house. In fact, after coming back to Christianity, he wrote, "Truth, wherever [it is found], belongs to [the] Lord."[1] But Augustine also came to see that his years growing up in the attic resulted in a jaundiced conception of Christianity. To see clearly, he would need to start over and open himself up to a new way of attending to the question of God.

In this and the following chapters, we hope to mimic Augustine's approach. In *Confessions* we see how, after leaving his ancient version of the attic, Augustine inhabited different spaces outside the Christian house. Having lived within these different residences, he saw what made each initially attractive, and he even recognized the abiding wisdom of certain features. But from his vantage point on the inside, he also came to see both structural flaws and problems of trying to live within the structures. Inspired by Augustine's approach, and keeping in mind Lewis's imagery of looking at and looking along, we begin by stepping inside of Richard Dawkins's New Atheism.

An Angry Atheism

If you grew up in the attic, New Atheism—the headline-grabbing group that peaked in the early 2000s—is almost certainly the stance you were most often warned about. But as we mentioned in the previous chapter, while the New Atheists land in a different home than those in the attic, their posture can look surprisingly similar: either "clench your teeth, react, and ridicule" or "lean over, focus narrowly, and achieve 'certainty.'"

Nevertheless, it is a mistake to imagine most atheists as card-carrying New Atheists, ready to unload scorn and mockery on the religious. As long as people aren't hurting others, most atheists don't particularly care what others believe. Even so, while much of the academic debate on the question of God has moved beyond the polemical frame set up by the New Atheists, many of their arguments still hang in the air and are revoiced by those jumping out of the attic—sometimes with flashes of anger reminiscent of the New Atheists themselves. Many of the deconversion accounts we have heard mention concerns about the relationship between Christianity and modern science, and Richard Dawkins perhaps has done more than any other person to advance the idea that one must choose between the two.

Famous for his dismissive approach to all religion, Dawkins has made it part of his life's mission to transform as many theists into atheists as he can. In this sense he is an evangelistic atheist. When Dawkins writes his books, he hopes "religious readers who open

[them] will be atheists when they put [them] down."[2] New Atheism frames itself as a counternarrative built around the rejection of all religious belief.

One of the most jarring aspects of Dawkins's work is his open disgust of religious believers, not just the leaders of religious organizations. He regularly states that believers are simply unintelligent. He explains that his books are written, in part, for those "whose native intelligence is strong enough to overcome [religious teaching]."[3] According to him, religious teaching is brainwashing, and only certain people are smart or lucky enough to snap out of religious belief.

For Dawkins, religion is not a harmless fantasy; it is a damaging delusion. In his view religions teach their adherents to blindly follow the dictates of religious leaders, shutting down independent thought. He even describes faith as a "mental illness" leading people to throw aside their natural reason in order to place their lives in the hands of arbitrary rules and teachings.[4] For Dawkins, the Christian faith is worse than blindness, for it actively turns believers away from scientific evidence.

Dawkins thinks "the God Hypothesis is a scientific hypothesis about the universe, which should be analyzed as skeptically as any other."[5] Of course, he finds this God Hypothesis to be wholly unconvincing. Since a god capable of creating the world has to be more complicated than the world he creates, any appeal to that god simply moves one further away from an effective hypothesis. If you need a creator to explain this complicated world, then who made the god that created this universe? Why propose a solution that leads to a more complicated problem than the one you began with?

Dawkins thinks atheism should be the default. After all, he reasons, atheism is simply the lack of belief in a god. Perhaps religious beliefs were reasonable a few centuries ago, but for the New Atheists, the explanatory power they once provided is now unneeded. As Dawkins sees it, religion used to serve the purpose of explaining the universe and our role in it. But science has rendered religion unnecessary. What religion once did through superstition, science now achieves through objective verifiable processes.[6] If religious claims were real, Dawkins argues, there would be a way to study them scientifically. Since no religion has put forward verifiable data and experiments to prove itself, Dawkins sees no reason to believe in any religion.

Where, then, for Dawkins, does the evidence lead us? What kind of universe does this evidence tell us we inhabit? Somewhere that few people will find appealing.

> In a universe of electrons and selfish genes, blind physical forces and genetic replication, some people are going to get hurt, other people are going to get lucky, and you won't find any rhyme or reason in it, nor any justice. The universe that we observe has precisely the properties we should expect if there is, at bottom, no design, no purpose, no evil, no good, nothing but pitiless indifference.[7]

The New Atheists see any kind of spiritual belief as faulty thinking. The sum total of reality is reducible to physics, and if something isn't directly tied to the causal relations of particles, it simply isn't real.[8]

Faith is a misfiring of brain synapses. Justice as we know it is a fiction. Love is nothing more than brain chemistry with purely functional purposes. There is no inherent meaning in the universe, and everything that exists is simply accidental. Eventually, science will be able to explain everything about reality, and anything that science cannot explain is imaginary.

Looking *At* and *Along* New Atheism

Each space outside the house of faith can teach us important lessons. We hope that, as in the case of Augustine, exploring the residences outside the house will help us ask better questions of the Christian tradition. After all, if the main floor of the house is worth wagering on, it should be able to handle whatever scrutiny we offer the places outside the house.

In the case of New Atheism, if someone embraces the kind of blind faith that leads to an outright rejection of modern science and human progress, Dawkins's critique should be sobering. As we talked about in part 1, attic Christianity has overreached in a number of ways. Some within the attic have grown downright skeptical of modern science and have demanded the kind of ideological conformity that Dawkins seems quite sensitive to. This may be why some in the attic, in particular, are still so focused on the New Atheists while many other Christians and academics have moved on. The critique Dawkins lays out against religion may be a strawman for most of Christianity, but it actually hits the attic. Yet perhaps part of what we can learn from the New Atheist anger toward religion is that religious beliefs can (and do) cause problems when built because of fear and resentment. With that being said, there are three reasons why we find that Dawkins's approach to religion is not as persuasive as he imagines.

First, Dawkins's position tilts at windmills. Like Don Quixote, Dawkins imagines himself in a fantastical battle. He sees faith as a fierce giant threatening the forward movement of science, as a mindless venture that eradicates independent thought; faith "is belief in spite of, even perhaps because of, the lack of evidence."[9]

His former Oxford University colleague Alister McGrath points out the problem with this definition:

> This, I must stress, is Dawkins' definition of faith, and it bears no resemblance to what Christians believe. It's on the same level as saying that the theory of evolution is about giraffes wanting to reach the leafy higher branches of trees, so that their necks stretch as a result. It's an amusing caricature of the real thing.[10]

As we have said, Dawkins's definition of faith does accurately represent the way some people in the attic practice Christianity. But their posture is not solely the result of their faith. It is likely the product of a complex network of sociological factors that happen to find fertile soil in religious fundamentalism.

Countless Christian thinkers and scientists besides McGrath implicitly call Dawkins's definition into question. Robert Boyle, a Christian theologian, was the world's first modern chemist. Georges

Lemaître, a Belgian Catholic priest, first proposed the Big Bang theory. Antonie Philips van Leeuwenhoek, the father of microbiology, was a Dutch Calvinist who saw his discoveries as evidence of God's handiwork. In fact, a survey of twentieth-century Nobel laureates showed that 65 percent of all recipients identified as Christian. An additional 20 percent identified as Jewish. It might surprise those who have bought into Dawkins's definition of religious faith that only 11 percent of all Nobel laureates identified as atheist or agnostic.[11] Now, there are significant sociological factors at play in these numbers—namely, that there are many more Christians in the world than there are atheists; it makes sense that Christians would be receiving more awards. We are not arguing that Christians are better scientists or more intelligent than their atheist counterparts. Rather, we are pointing out that it's simply untrue that religious belief impedes scientific progress.

Second, Dawkins's position impoverishes our view of life. If Dawkins refined his critique to apply specifically to people who reject scientific advancement, his works would be more reasonable. But by maintaining his sweeping and misapplied definition, he ends up critiquing far more. In casting everything outside the causal interactions of physics as rubbish superstition, he catches much of our modern thought-world in the crossfire. While the target of his assault is religion, his critiques implicitly frame the humanities as being equally irrelevant.[12] If only the natural sciences reveal truth, then what do we do with our study of law? Psychology? English? Each of these fields claim sources of truth that do not fit within Dawkins's view of life.

The convictions that we bring to the table when thinking about the nature of the universe fundamentally shape the range of options we will consider. This is one of the reasons Dawkins presents materialism as the default assumption. If he can insist you begin your search for truth by assuming reality is mindless matter, then the onus is on religion to demonstrate—through the use of natural science—how there is more to the universe. But this is an impossible task; by definition, faith invokes something *beyond* natural science.

Materialism itself cannot be verified through scientific processes. No one can prove that my love for my child is real. Most intuitively understand that love exists and justice matters. In forcing everything to be explained at the level of biology and particles, Dawkins excludes the most significant things in our lives, including values, meaning, beauty, and perhaps even the reliability of cognitive faculties themselves.

Lewis argues that a world like the one Dawkins imagines would make our common intuitions about truth suspect. "If there is nothing but Nature, . . . reason must have come into existence by a historical process."[13] This historical process would be evolution, and it would have slowly refined human brains to create "reason" as a means of increasing the chances of reproduction (since reason isn't a reality independent of human perception in a materialistic world). Yet there is no compelling reason to believe that "reason" as a cognitive function increases survival rates. As Alvin Plantinga has argued, in the universe Dawkins imagines we would have reason to trust our rational capacity *only* when our conclusions would directly shape our actions in such a way that they increased our chances of survival on the path to reproduction. Since evolution would select belief-producing faculties that promoted survivability—as opposed to selecting faculties that promoted truth knowing—we would have no justifiable reason to trust our minds to produce true beliefs. It's telling that "Nietzsche, Nagel, Stroud, Churchland, and Darwin, nontheists all, seem to concur: (naturalistic) evolution gives one reason to doubt that human cognitive faculties produce for the most part true beliefs."[14] The world Dawkins imagines—which combines both atheistic naturalism and evolution—puts abstract reasoning on shaky ground.

In addition to abstract reasoning, moral truths that so many people in the modern world accept on principle are called into question if we follow Dawkins's path. For example, Martin Luther King Jr.'s assertion that "the arc of the moral universe is long but it bends toward justice" is nonsense if science is our only source of truth.[15] What is the moral universe? What is justice?

Most people, including the nonreligious, believe that nonmaterial things, like morality and compassion, are significant. Nonreligious people sometimes punt this contradiction by invoking a vague appeal to "mystery," but Dawkins cannot do that. "'Mystery' [is] a category which [Dawkins] cheerfully, if a little prematurely, reduces to 'plain insanity or surrealist nonsense.' . . . Religious people who talk about 'mystery' are just irrational mystics who are too lazy or frightened to use their minds properly."[16] Dawkins's dismissal of mystery is perhaps the clearest example of the extreme confidence he has in his position. Try as he might, it is doubtful he will ever banish the reality of mystery from the human experience.

Third, Dawkins overpromises and underdelivers on his claims. The non-Christian philosopher Mary Midgley points out that "Dawkins' claim to know that there is no [purposeful cause of the universe] is just as grand—just as overconfident—a conclusion as any positive claim that there is one. Extreme negative proposals need just as much support as positive ones."[17] Dawkins does not provide support for his extreme negative assertions. He asserts them and expects you to believe them. If you don't, well, then you're probably brainwashed.

A more realistic take comes from Charles Darwin, an intellectual giant for Dawkins. Darwin recognized the reasonable intuitions that lead people to become theists—namely, the difficulty of imagining our complex world arising from pure chance and the existential difficulty of believing that all we know is headed toward oblivion.[18] Unlike Darwin, Dawkins does his argument a great disservice by waving away people's intuitions toward faith—and the questions that fuel them—with smug condescension.

After all, where did matter come from? Does nonbeing evolve into being? Does a fine-tuned universe arise by chance? Does intelligence really come from non-intelligence? Does consciousness emerge from nonconsciousness? Many of the arguments you might have heard growing up that seek to demonstrate God's existence are built on deep-seated human intuitions that lurk behind these questions. And while critics often point out, rightly, that these arguments do not prove without a doubt the Christian God's existence, they are nonetheless rooted in a powerful set of intuitions that grate against the claims of naturalists like Dawkins. This is perhaps partly why studies show that humans, even children from secular societies, are naturally inclined to believe in some kind of deity. The evidence suggests the "natural" state for humans is to believe in the divine; it takes specific and—historically speaking—unique cultural conditions for groups to begin to believe otherwise.[19]

Consider moral obligation, the belief that we as humans have a duty to behave in certain ways. Moral obligations include basic imperatives that we teach our children, such as "You should not murder or steal; you should treat people fairly." The atheist Luc Ferry admits that he "cannot invent . . . the imperatives of the moral life" and yet they seem to "impose themselves on [him] as if they [came] from elsewhere."[20] And these imperatives are not simply cultural obligations imposed from the outside. If you traveled to a culture where murdering a minority group based on their ethnicity was accepted, or where the community permitted the habitual mistreatment of women, you would probably still object—strongly. So, if an atheist were to accept moral obligation without making a blind leap of faith, where might they ground it? In science?

So far, the scientific quest to ground morality has essentially failed.[21] Three dominant paradigms have been proposed to explain morality on the basis of science. "Sentimentalism" explains morality on the basis of feelings, "utilitarianism" bases morality on maximizing pleasure and minimizing pain, and "evolutionary ethics" roots morality in the processes of evolutionary selection.[22]

Each of these approaches has had varied success in describing the observable phenomenon of morality. None of them, however, have been able to build a reliable set of moral standards. In fact, "after five hundred years of scientific inquiry into the nature of morality, the most trustworthy scientific findings at best [describe morality or its origins]."[23] Even more problematically, there are no scientific findings that have come close to providing moral obligations.[24] Science can observably tell us, "Many humans have been racist or sexist, and here are some ways you might curtail racism." But science cannot tell us that racism is inherently wrong. Since science is fundamentally tied to the job of describing natural phenomena, it has no resources for differentiating which parts of natural processes are good and which parts are bad. Unless you are able to do something that more than five centuries worth of scientific inquiry has not been able to do, you won't succeed in providing an answer to those questions in scientific terms. Science can tell us how to achieve certain ends, but it cannot tell us what those ends should be.

Avoiding the Attic of New Atheism

Dawkins's position turns on one central claim: only that which is scientifically verifiable should be trusted. If there is no scientific proof that God exists, then one should assume that he does not. But if you try to hold this stance consistently, you will find it unlivable. It pits religion against science in a way that does not fit the history of science. It disregards religion's explanatory power. It pressures people to ignore powerful intuitions. And it fundamentally misunderstands the claim of Christianity and the nature of faith. Belief in God, similar to many other widespread human beliefs, can be justified, but Christianity does not claim that God is a hypothesis that can be proven through a scientific experiment. Its claims have to be explored and tested in other ways.

Dawkins critiques Christians for their faith, but he operates from his own attic-like space. As McGrath has pointed out, "Dawkins is obliged to make a 'leap of faith' from agnosticism to atheism."[25] The assertion that there is no God, no ultimate meaning, no ultimate significance, and no ultimate justice in the universe is a bold claim. It is certainly not what many would consider common sense.

Nevertheless, we should avoid thinking most atheists harbor the type of animosity toward religion that Dawkins and other leading New Atheists have displayed. In fact, most ex-attic dwellers, even those who have absorbed some of the New Atheists' polemics, eventually opt for different quarters. In our next chapter we will explore a more sanguine residence where many ex-attic-dwelling atheists and agnostics choose to reside.

7

Optimistic Skepticism

THE SCHOLAR BART EHRMAN'S popular writings are often framed by his journey from fundamentalist Christianity to agnosticism. By his own telling, Ehrman began losing faith in the Bible while attending graduate school. Over time his misgivings turned into major problems. His journey is told as a coming-of-age story of hard-earned unbelief, culminating in his facing the fact that the Bible probably isn't what he had long thought it was. For Ehrman, "the floodgates opened," and he came to see the Bible as a "very human book" filled with errors.[1]

While Ehrman's departure from his earlier views certainly shook him, it wasn't the breaking point. That came when he "could no longer explain how there can be a good and all-powerful God actively involved with this world, given the state of things."[2] We find much to empathize with in Ehrman's struggle with the problem of evil. In some ways we've even come close to agreeing with him.

We aren't startled when people admit they can't answer the problem of evil. In fact, the more we have reflected on human suffering and evil, the more we are taken aback when someone claims they *can*. Often, the way those in the attic approach the question shirks its difficulties. In trying to justify God they overreach and justify too much. When an "answer" to the problem of evil does that, we find ourselves responding with Ehrman-like skepticism. But there are different forms of skepticism, even Christian forms. Alvin Plantinga, one of the most important Christian philosophers of the twentieth century, says Christians *shouldn't* claim to know the answer to the problem of evil. In his own words: "Christians don't, nor do other believers in God, as far as I know, really know why God permits evil."[3]

We will have more to say on that shortly, but there's an important observation to make about the first part of Ehrman's deconversion story. In it Ehrman takes a similar posture to the Bible that he takes to the problem of evil. It's a posture that for many people feels intuitive, even obvious—so obvious, in fact, that they become insufficiently skeptical of their own skepticism. In fact, sometimes the quickest minds, and the confidence that often accompanies great intellect, can shield their owners from their blind spots.

A More Fitting Posture

People commonly assume that if God exists, all his cards are on the table. With confidence in our cognitive powers, we late moderns assume there is no divine idea that we should not be able to grasp. Notably, Christians living in the attic can display a similar overconfidence in their ability to answer the whys of evil. You've probably seen it yourself. The preacher strides up to the pulpit and claims to have the answer to evil. His answer is tidy, and it makes his Christian audience feel good, heightening their expectations; they imagine the expert apologists have solved the problem. But one day some begin to grow out of such "solutions." And rightly so.

This misplaced confidence in our own capacity to reach into the heavens is one of the unique features of our modern world. Evil and suffering are old problems. Previous societies wrestled with them emotionally and intellectually. Yet their struggles led to lament, confusion, even angry accusations, but not widespread unbelief. Just read through Job or the Psalms. These authors doubted and wrestled with God, but their suffering didn't lead them to deny

God existed. That did not happen until, as the philosopher Charles Taylor explains, the modern world began to believe its own press.[4] We now assume that analyzing and deciphering the cosmic stage should lead us to solve the problem. So, if there is a god and he has reasons for permitting evil, we expect them to be intelligible to us. If not, then it's, as Ehrman's book is titled, "God's problem."

Ancient Christians, and, in fact, most people in human history, assumed the world was enchanted, naturally believed God and his ways to be mysterious, and knew the dangers of intellectual pride. In all the Bible's wondrous diversity—from Genesis 1, to Job, to the Gospels and the other New Testament writings—Scripture tells readers to be humble before a God who is well beyond our ken.[5]

Ehrman notes there are Christians who take this more skeptical approach to the problem of evil, but he doesn't engage them meaningfully. He explores Job and Ecclesiastes but vacillates in his takeaways. On the one hand, he says "we should take a lesson from" the author of Ecclesiastes's confession that "he doesn't know" and that "despite all our attempts, suffering sometimes defies explanation." Yet, in response to the book of Job, he dismisses God's revelation of himself without an explanation of why Job suffered as a "cop out."[6]

What one considers satisfying will vary from person to person. But for us, a response that takes human limits seriously will grapple with our experiences of evil and will refuse to require of Christianity what Christianity does not claim to provide. A response like this is more satisfying than any other we've heard. The closest Ehrman comes to this is in his introduction, where he mentions the views of some of his "brilliant friends":

> In its most nuanced form (and for these friends everything is extremely nuanced), this view is that religious faith is not an intellectualizing system for explaining everything. Faith is a mystery and an experience of the divine in the world, not a solution to a set of problems.
>
> I respect this view deeply and some days I wish I shared it. But I don't.[7]

After spending so much time critiquing positions he finds so reprehensible, why doesn't Ehrman spend more time engaging this position he respects? If Ehrman is willing to admit that the Bible repeatedly calls for this humble posture, and if he respects people who embody it, why isn't he willing to interact with it more?

A Contradictory or Multilayered Response?

It seems Ehrman doesn't share his friends' more nuanced position due to one of his central contentions: the Bible has so many *other* responses to evil—responses that Ehrman believes contradict each other. Ehrman describes the Bible as offering five different responses:

> "Suffering comes from God as a punishment against sin."
> "Suffering is the result of human beings sinning against other human beings."
> "Suffering is redemptive."
> "Suffering is a test of faith."
> "Suffering is at times mysterious."[8]

This is where Ehrman's posture toward the Bible spills over into conclusions about God. For Ehrman pits these biblical responses against each other, but he needn't. Nothing demands that we read the Bible this way, and we see no good reason to expect the biblical authors to always give the same response to a complicated question. Ancient readers certainly didn't expect sacred texts to work this way. Many of the biblical authors are aware of and respect the broader textual tradition, aiming to expand and layer responses to weighty concepts like evil and suffering. In doing so they offer a web of responses, framed in particular ways for particular communities, that speak to the complexity of evil. We find this to be one of the Bible's richest features, allowing it to speak in a profound way to different people facing different situations at different times. As Christopher Watkin describes, the biblical responses are "reductive if treated in isolation, but when they are woven together in the biblical canon, . . . they provide a rich, complex, and existentially authentic view of the world."[9]

In short, expectations matter. What if you simply have the wrong expectations of the Bible (expectations that are sometimes inherited from the attic and remain intact long after a person has moved on)? However, if you read the Scriptures from the perspective of the main floor of Christianity and give up wrong expectations of how the Bible should work, you might just discover the rich and layered responses you need. This is what has happened to both of us. The more we have studied the Bible, the more we have come to see it as offering rich and nuanced responses to life's most important questions. Like a wise teacher, the Bible favors textured responses over rote answers, and its responses are intelligible to children yet brimming with enough nuance and depth to hold the attention of even the most brilliant mind—if received with the appropriate posture.

A Logical Response

Now we are ready to consider the logic of the classic problem of evil head on.

> God is all-powerful.
> God is all-loving.
> There is suffering.

After surveying the responses to this problem, Ehrman concludes that an all-powerful and all-loving God cannot exist alongside suffering. Since he couldn't explain how all three could be true, he left the faith.

As "skeptical theists" (yes, that's a thing), we offer a reply in the form of a fourth premise. According to the Bible, neither God nor his ways can be fully known by humans. The biblical authors assume God is infinite and humans are finite. Christianity has long said that God is omnipotent and good, there is suffering, *and* God's ways transcend our understanding. The fourth premise changes the conclusion.

The philosopher John Wykstra compares our inability to see no-see-ums (a tiny fly not visible to the naked eye) with our ability to see a large dog. If I were standing beside you and said, "Look at that giant dog right in front of you," and you did not see anything, you would have an intellectual warrant to reject my claim. However, if I said, "There are no-see-ums in front of you," you would not have reason to reject or accept my claim. Who knows whether they're there? Likewise, if God is the God revealed in the Christian Scriptures, we have "good reasons to think that if there were God-purposed goods for sufferings . . . these would often be beyond our ken."[10]

You might not consider this an answer to the problem. If by "answer" you mean that it must explain all the whys of suffering, then we agree with you. But Christianity never makes such lofty claims about human knowledge. Instead, the Bible gives us good reasons to think that knowing *all* the reasons is "beyond our ken."

This is why the philosopher John Cottingham is right to say:

> To believe in God is not to be able to explain why terrible things happen, and why many lives are ruined or tragically cut short. The message of the book of Job is absolutely clear on this point: there is no explanation, or no explanation we can comprehend. To be a believer is not to "solve" this problem, but is something else entirely. It is to hold that the meaning and purpose of our lives . . . is to live in accordance with the "sacred" requirements of justice and compassion. To believe in God . . . is to believe that we are required, by a holy and inviolable power not of ourselves, to do what is right and to avoid what is wrong.[11]

Not Skeptical Enough

If you leave behind these misguided expectations when exiting the attic, you might just discover compelling reasons to stay in the Christian house.

In the closing chapter of *God's Problem*, Ehrman analyzes Fyodor Dostoevsky's acclaimed novel *The Brothers Karamazov*. Ehrman takes up the argument of Ivan, one of the titular brothers and a skeptical intellectual, who impresses his listeners with devastating critiques of the philosophical overreach exhibited by some Christians. Ehrman frames Ivan as a rational hero. Yet Dostoevsky, himself both an Orthodox Christian and a skeptic of glib answers offered in the face of the human plight, meant Ivan's brother Alyosha, not Ivan, to be the character who inspires imitation. Alyosha never keeps pace with Ivan intellectually, but he is the only brother in the story who is able to flourish in the midst of suffering and tragedy. Ivan's position bears a logical appeal, and he does defeat attic-like Christian answers, but Dostoevsky uses the logic of the narrative to show that Ivan's view undermines both itself and the human experience. After all, by the end of the novel, Ivan loses his mind. Dostoevsky's novel challenges the hardened rationalists of his day to be more skeptical about *their skepticism*. If you are tempted to bypass grappling with Ivan's failure to live out his own rejection of God without the walls of existential dread closing in on him, it might mean you aren't looking closely enough at what it is like to reside in this form of skepticism. Ehrman's silence toward this central point of Dostoevsky's book might reveal more than he intends.

Lewis, for example, once rejected Christianity along lines similar to Ehrman's and Ivan's. Yet Lewis later saw that his problem with evil was itself a problem that his atheism couldn't explain. "My argument against God was that the universe seemed so cruel and unjust. But how had I got this idea of *just* and *unjust*? A man does not call a line crooked unless he has some idea of a straight line. What was I comparing this universe with when I called it unjust?"[12]

In other words, the fact that evil is a problem that perplexes, repulses, and angers seems to gesture to something beyond us. Given the deep intuition that the world *shouldn't* be like this, have you ever asked yourself why it is that you feel it shouldn't be? Why would we expect a world of nothing more than matter and energy to be anything other than absurd and violent? Why do we struggle so fiercely against the reality of the way things are?

Like Lewis, if we go so far as to reject God on the basis of evil, we are intuitively bearing witness that we believe in some kind of standard by which to judge the universe. It might just be that buried beneath your skeptical doubts you can find reasons not to leave the main floor of the Christian house. For not only does Christianity proclaim a moral universe that provides a foundation for these intuitions, but it also provides resources for what our present society is perhaps most lacking: the ability to face evil and live through suffering without surrendering to the worst of human tendencies. And this is no small consolation, for as the University of Columbia professor Andrew Delbanco has observed, today "a gulf has opened up in our culture between the visibility of evil and the intellectual resources available for coping with it."[13]

A Cruel Optimism

Critiquing comes pretty easy for most of us; offering a consistent and livable alternative isn't so easy. And since we need a livable space, consider not just what you might be leaving behind if you leave the Christian house but also what you might be jumping into.

To draw on what Delbanco has said about our culture's lack of intellectual resources, does Ehrman's agnosticism give us ways to cope with evil and suffering?

Ehrman believes "this life is all there is."[14] But he doesn't find this to be an "occasion for despair and despondency"; instead, as he puts it, this "should be a source of joy and dreams—joy of living for the moment and dreams of trying to make the world a better place, both for ourselves and for others in it."

On the next page he continues:

> I think we should work hard to make the world—the one we live in—the most pleasing place it can be for ourselves. We should love and be loved. We should cultivate our friendships, enjoy our intimate relationships, cherish our family lives. We should make money and spend money. The more the better. We should enjoy good food and drink. We should eat out and order unhealthy desserts, and we should cook steaks on the grill and drink Bordeaux. We should walk around the block, work in the garden, watch basketball, and drink

beer. We should travel and read books and go to museums and look at art and listen to music. We should drive nice cars and have nice homes. We should make love, have babies, and raise families. We should do what we can to love life—it's a gift and it will not be with us for long.

But we should also work hard to make our world the most pleasing place it can be *for others*. . . . We need to live life to its fullest and help others as well to enjoy the fruits of the land.[15]

Sound familiar? Montaigne, whom we met in chapter 3, would be pleased to see his advice being followed five hundred years later. Ehrman urges an unvarnished pursuit of immanent contentment.

We will explore further problems with this approach to life in several later chapters. For now we note that Ehrman's advice offers measly resources for practically living out the ethics, fortitude, and joy that he commends. It offers no moral grounding for why someone should feel obligated to live the kind of moral life he describes. The first part of his vision—enjoying life by way of nice cars, homes, and food—will inevitably be in tension with his charge to help others. While we share his moral sensibility—that we *should* care for others—why do so if it requires us to give up time spent in our own gardens or if it prevents us from working the overtime required to move into a nicer neighborhood? Ehrman never gives a motivating rationale for putting others over self.

And if Ehrman is correct in saying that this world is all there is, then one should be willing to look realistically at what it means to live consistently in this space before moving in. What does this mean for those who can't enjoy cars and fine wines? What does this mean for those who enjoy such luxuries but are crippled with dull emptiness or anxious restlessness? What does this mean for the person in hospice care with a terminal diagnosis?

The clouds of suffering and loss, which Ehrman reminds us of so powerfully, cast dark shadows over the "gift" of life Ehrman encourages us to enjoy. But if Ehrman is correct, if we are alone in the cosmos, then we need to face the fact that his good news rings hollow. Instead of proclaiming the "joy" to be found in the news that this life is all there is, as Francis Spufford has put it, he might as well have said, "There's no help coming."[16]

Spufford calls upon Augustine to unmask the shallowness of asserting that this kind of skepticism could foster joy: "It amounts to a denial of hope or consolation, on any but the most chirpy, squeaky, bubble-gummy reading of the human situation. St. Augustine called this kind of thing 'cruel optimism' fifteen hundred years ago, and it's still cruel."[17]

Spufford is not alone. Many people who leave the attic aren't settling for this space with Ehrman. Like Lewis, they recognize the intuitions lying beneath their revulsion toward evil. They can't shake the feeling that this world is not as it should be, but they also recognize that this deep-seated intuition isn't rational unless there is some kind of standard beyond this world. They also can't so easily reconcile the idea that this life is all there is with the claim that there is nothing to be frightened of. And like Ehrman, they sense that life is a gift. But where does the gift come from if not a giver? For these reasons, they opt for another residence altogether—such as the one we will explore in our next chapter.

8

Open Spirituality

RECENTLY THE YOUTUBE PERSONALITY and cohost of *Good Mythical Morning* Rhett McLaughlin shared his deconversion story online. Rhett grew up in conservative church circles, but after college he began to grow uncomfortable with Christianity. He is thoughtful about his pilgrimage out of the faith, and since he is so familiar with Christian terminology and thought, he is capable of explaining his new beliefs, what we're calling "open spirituality," in a way that makes sense to Christians in the midst of deconstruction.

Rhett's rejection of Christianity is multifaceted. He was deeply involved in a Christian subculture and even spent time as a "professional Christian," working for a campus ministry. He grew up in the attic, and the specter of that upper room shapes his rejection of Christianity. Three aspects of his new outlook toward life stand out.

First, Rhett isn't a hard-and-fast atheist or naturalist. Instead, he "[sees] spirituality as an openness to things that transcend [his] conceptual understanding." You won't hear him lob clichés about religion poisoning everything. In fact, he sees religion as a necessary part of life; he doesn't think "religious unaffiliation" is something that most people can sustain. Most people have, in Rhett's view, some innate need for a spiritual dimension—though it is mysterious and hard to define. We appreciate Rhett's sensitivity to the sacred, which distinguishes his residence from the previous two.

For those who reside in open spirituality, each person ends up picking whatever aspects of religion help them connect with the sacred. The real danger in religion, says Rhett, is the *certainty* it cultivates, or at least the appearance of certainty. For Rhett, Christianity claimed to be a "ship on the ocean of uncertainty," but that certainty "was an illusion." After he jumped off the ship, he didn't feel swept away in uncertainty; he felt free.[1] Rhett still longs for something transcendent, but he is repulsed by the restrictive nature of most organized religions. Rhett wants an enchanted world, but he is skeptical of the specific truth claims of narrow systems that box in the mysteries of the sacred. As a response to attic Christianity, this makes a lot of sense. (However, as we will see in part 3, main-floor Christianity has plenty of space for mystery, but with an ancient and weather-tested frame.)

Second, Rhett still believes that morality transcends culture, tribe, and person, though he is unsure about the source of this universal morality (we'll return to that in the final section of this chapter). In many ways he is still committed to the moral teachings of Jesus. In fact, a major reason he rejected Christianity was that Christians have failed to live up to their proclaimed morals. Rhett explains that he experienced far too much complicity with racism in the church and that white evangelicals had been so preoccupied with protecting their own freedoms that they had failed to care for hurting members of society. In a particularly expressive moment, Rhett explains that young people are leaving Christianity because they have "[developed] a sense for truth and justice." They have "read the words of Jesus. And they got it. . . . They are not leaving because they don't know the truth. They are leaving because they do."

This brings us to a third aspect of Rhett's perspective: he senses the goodness and beauty in many of Jesus's teachings, "regardless of the historicity of Jesus." In his view Christianity is a human attempt to systematize the mysterious transcendent world, so Christ's existence and the accuracy of his recorded words don't really matter. If they are a collection of human words that were, over time, shaped to express this inner longing, then they can be valid without being historically true. In other words, he avoids the historical particulars of Christianity while accepting the abstract spirituality it gestures to. Rhett appreciates portions of Scripture while distancing himself from parts he doesn't agree with. Christianity contains many good and beautiful ideas, but Jesus is not "the way and the truth and the life" (John 14:6), he never rose from the dead, and he is not coming back.

We highlight Rhett as the exemplar for this stance because of his openness, vulnerability, and relatability. As we listened to his story, we found ourselves sympathizing with many of his concerns and sharing many of the same critiques. And as Rhett would tell you, he is still "in process." He has not committed himself to holding any particular beliefs rigidly, and he wants to be open to discovering new perspectives.

However, we think the attic, rather than the house, is the source of much of Rhett's disillusionment with Christianity. The following critiques are aimed at the general position of open spirituality rather than at Rhett in particular. Rhett has never presented his stance formally, and some of our critiques may not apply to him. Nonetheless, we think they do apply to open spirituality quite well.

Too Comfortable?

Many who have jumped out of the window find themselves living in open spirituality. It allows them freedom to build their own beliefs, such as the existence of an afterlife or the eternal significance of love, without what feels like the confining walls of religion. This is an understandably attractive space for many people. But before you make yourself comfortable here, we ask that you be as critical of this residence as you have been of the attic you grew up in.

First, consider what is going on behind the scenes. This position is based on the rejection of established religious structures. Instead of trusting the basics of a tradition or historical faith, individuals play the role of a judge, sifting through various belief systems and weighing their merits. Ultimately, they assess their strengths and weaknesses, taking only the best pieces with them. They do not need to tie themselves to historical standards, because they can choose what is right and wrong through self-reflection. By positioning themselves this way, they seek to attain a freedom of belief. Each person is Caesar in the coliseum of their own faith, and only when the evaluation produces a thumbs-up will a belief survive. This is how many people approach faith today. After all, each of us must think critically about what to believe, right? So, shouldn't each person decide for themselves what they believe? In some sense, yes. But there is a difference between, on the one hand, stepping into a faith that has been tried and tested for a couple of millennia and, on the other hand, attempting to cobble things together as you go. Ask yourself, if you are the emperor of belief, what makes you think you should have that kind of confidence in yourself?

This do-it-yourself approach appears even more perilous when you reflect on how we humans form beliefs. Consider the scene from the movie *Gladiator* when Russell Crowe's character harnesses the crowd's energy to coerce the emperor into giving him a thumbs-up, despite the emperor's hatred of him. This is somewhat like what happens to us, except in the subtle arena of our minds, the crowd doesn't force our hand but rather converts our perceptions and bends our vision until we see the world a certain way. We humans can't help looking to others for standards and values. In this way our modern social environment doesn't just provide a smorgasbord of religious options; it also shapes the assumptions and values that guide the choices we make.

"Self-choice as an ideal," Charles Taylor explains, "makes sense only because some *issues* are more significant than others."[2] But individuals cannot determine what is significant on their own. Communities decide what is significant. Taylor offers the example of someone claiming she is significant because she has 3,732 hairs on her head or is "exactly the same height as some tree on the Siberian plain." Those claims to significance feel odd. That is because no one assigns significance individually—"as though people could determine what is significant, either by decision, or perhaps unwittingly, by just feeling that way."[3]

If you see yourself as looking at all the different options, picking and choosing what you will take from Christianity, you're reflecting the priorities of our modern world. It's an experience that would seem foreign, even shocking, to people of almost any other time and place. But we feel at ease picking and choosing what beliefs are best for us. In fact, self-choosing is an assumed ideal. The crowd has taught us to value individual choice over conformity.

Don't misunderstand our point: we aren't advocating for rote conformity. The problem is not personal choice per se. Instead, the danger is the very real risk of recognizing *only* the surface reality of belief formation. When it comes to the coliseum of personal belief, the crowd provides the communal narratives that help form our values. While Christians and adherents of other religious traditions are also shaped by communal scripts (narratives we assume and see ourselves playing a role in), those in the open spirituality space are often unaware that they are too. Nonetheless, these scripts, operating behind the scenes, serve as a compass for people's hearts and minds, guiding their decisions about what should be rejected as irrational, denied as bad, or embraced as good.

The Sunday school stories learned during childhood have been abandoned, only to be replaced by a new set of meaning-laden stories. And if the moral visions of these tales are tacitly working without being scrutinized, they are all the more potent. This leads us to a key question: For the person who has embraced open spirituality, what does this compass point them to? And what are the underlying assumptions of these new cultural narratives?

For over half a century scholars have been tracing the historically unique—and we must emphasize that these are truly unique, even if they seem natural and universal—features of our late-modern context:

- The defining ideal value of our age is that each person is called individually to cast off external norms and find the true "you."[4]

- The functional moral stance assumes that what is right should be rooted in personal values and subjective emotional sentiment.[5]
- Self-actualization or feeling better about oneself is prized over and against seeking religious salvation and conforming one's life to formal, external standards.[6]

This is the cultural air we have been breathing for over five decades. Notice that these assumptions have worked together to create a variety of different spiritual groups, which all share common sensibilities. Those who belong to this conglomerate of competing beliefs, which is connected by a substrate of common cultural assumptions, are labeled by Tara Isabella Burton as the "Remixed":

> Today's Remixed reject authority, institution, creed, and moral universalism. They value intuition, personal feeling, and experiences. They demand to rewrite their own scripts about how the universe, and human beings, operate. Shaped by the twin forces of a creative-communicative Internet and consumer capitalism, today's Remixed don't want to receive doctrine, to assent automatically to a creed. They want to choose—and more often than not, *purchase*—the spiritual path that feels more authentic, more meaningful, to them. They prioritize intuitional spirituality over institutional religion. And they want, when available institutional options fail to suit their needs, the freedom to mix and match, to create their own daily rituals and practices and belief systems.[7]

In other words: *the open spirituality space is not as "free" as it might seem. It mirrors the norms and values imbibed, narrated, marketed, and reinforced in a significant stream of our provincial cultural context.*

Open spirituality has different practices and scripts from those of the Christian attic you grew up in. But they are similar in some regards. Both are reactionary and are, to a large extent, blind to their own cultural situatedness. Marketers and internet activists are the new Sunday school teachers, making dogmatic and often historically unique claims and asking you to trust them. Indeed, you are "free" to decide for yourself. But your choices are guided by novel elements in the late-modern air that are carried along by stories, songs, and symbols and that form your values and guide your judgments about what should be believed and what should be doubted.

Again, don't misunderstand our point: the problem is *not* that we are formed by cultural artifacts, practices, and stories. This is an inescapable feature of personhood. The problem is that in leaving Christianity, you may think you now have the coliseum all to yourself, that you have a neutral view and are finally free from the controlling influence of religion. This simply isn't true, and it glosses over the deeper realities of how humans operate. People imagine they are following an inner spark or a commonsense picture of human flourishing for guidance. As comfortable as this explanation might be, it doesn't hold up under scrutiny. This new residence casts itself as freeing, but how do you know it isn't just a different kind of attic, with those in power hoping you will stay pacified and not ask too many uncomfortable questions?

Shallow Resources for Self-Critique

This first problem leads to a second: *open spirituality lacks the resources to provide the cultural distance needed for healthy self-critique.* In other words, open spirituality submits to tribal "gods," and you may not realize they demand sacrifice.

In the ancient world the pagan gods allowed—even encouraged—what amounts to sexual abuse by modern standards. It wasn't until the fifth century that a Christian emperor "enacted a law banning the use of coercion in the sex industry . . . to repress prostitution of slaves, daughters, and other vulnerable members of society, which was anything but a marginal part of the classical sexual order."[8] What we would consider abuse today was a feature, not a bug, of Greco-Roman society. As the classicist Kyle Harper has pointed out, "The moral foundations of the law [that prohibited these sexual violations] were, *there can be no doubt*, Christian."[9] It is a sad irony that Christianity launched a moral transformation now embedded in the West's deepest ethical aspirations only to see the church too often fail to confront such abuses.

Our aim is neither to suggest that those in this space would disagree with these moral aspirations nor to whitewash the failures of Christians. This is a historical example of how Christianity's universal claims—namely, that people are created by a good God and in his image—inspired ancient Christians to offer a clear-eyed critique of a cultural norm. On the other hand the cultural authorities and their local gods failed to make any critique and even propped up that particular norm. In a similar way open spirituality lacks a clear source that stands outside the cultural values it is reflecting. The person who adopts open spirituality is right to call Christians out for failing to live up to their own Christian standards. We join with them in this critique, even aiming it at our own lives. Yet those who have inhabited open spirituality have a real problem; they lack a clear, transcendent moral source outside of history. This leaves them with abstract and shifting moral preferences rather than a concrete moral grounding.

For example, in the 1970s many thought that sexual relationships between undergraduate students and their middle-aged professors were a form of sexual liberation. Now fast-forward to the era of the #MeToo movement. Given the power dynamics inherent in these campus sexual encounters, they are rightly seen as abusive. What was once liberation is now scorned. Or consider the growing disgust toward hookup culture.[10] Sex without commitment is considered problematic—maybe even a form of exploitation—to a growing number of young people today, but it was once seen as the path to flourishing by those in the sexual-liberation movement. A former rallying point for women's liberation is increasingly seen as a source of harm and disenfranchisement.

These moral shifts, however, are not the result of a call to submit to a newly discovered fabric of creation, as Christians would have it. They are the result of a call to submit to a social storytelling about well-being. The problem for the open spirituality space is that *the same kind* of social storytelling about the well-being was being told in the sixties and seventies. Social stories without a source outside the created order will lead adherents in circles. Open spirituality isn't grounded enough to break the cycle. For within this space there is no clear true north, and its adherents are therefore left with shifting sentiments of what does and doesn't *seem* good or bad at different moments. As a result, residing in open spirituality simply cannot provide a stable and sustainable vision of "the good life."

In contrast, Christians appeal to an ancient moral tradition—the Scriptures, the created order, and the revelation of Jesus Christ—which they have understood as the way God, who transcends history, speaks within history. The result is a morality that is, at times, uncomfortable. For some, the discomfort is caused by the idea of God offering forgiveness and mercy to people who continue to fail; for others, it is God's judgment; for others, it is a difficult and countercultural sexual ethic. Invariably, if we worship a God who stands over all of history, we should expect this God to push back on our culturally specific assumptions. We should expect such a God to make us uncomfortable and to challenge every culture on certain points.

The major turning points of the Christian story have remained pillars of the house of faith for two thousand years, providing a narrative structure with serious implications that Christians have had to wrestle with continually. In this way the narrative of God—his creation of the world as good, his making humans in his own image, the fall of humanity, the life of Jesus, and the new creation—furnishes the house with enduring features that allow people to critique and correct the problematic elements within the broader culture and the house itself. While it is true that Christians have often failed to live faithfully within this story, when they have rightly leaned into its pillars, they have stood up against moral distortions, bringing real reform to the church and to society.

Open spirituality, too, is framed by narratives. Stories, catechized into the human heart by way of everything from marketing to movies, tacitly furnish those who practice open spirituality with values and frame their daily experience. However, living within open spirituality means not having the same type of transcendent, moral source that the Christian house provides, with its stable and historically supported narrative. This difference shouldn't be taken lightly. Open spirituality's shortcoming leaves its inhabitants without a view by which they can adequately see and critique their own assumptions and, as we will see next, makes them vulnerable to the destructive forces of cultural storms.

The Need for More

None of this means that residents of open spirituality lack noble and passionate convictions. Most seek to live moral lives and care about their neighbors. But this leads us to our third concern: *open spirituality lacks the stable resources needed to support the highest ideals of its occupants.*

Take two values that we share with most who live within open spirituality: human dignity and universal benevolence.[11] Most societies have taken it for granted that people should be treated in unequal and even brutal ways. Slavery, infanticide, mistreatment of women, human sacrifice, and widow burning were common. Today, however, most of us assume that every person has equal dignity and that individuals have an obligation to love others. But neither experience nor science can generate such towering moral obligations. Does open spirituality provide the rational grounding and practical motivation to sustain these convictions?

Let's start with rational grounding. By this we don't mean "Can people who inhabit open spirituality hold to these high moral ideals?" Of course they can. The question is whether open spirituality has a rational moral foundation for these ideals.

Some suggest that these convictions are common sense. After all, if we all live by these ideals, it will make the cultural conditions better for everyone. As Christian Smith, a sociologist at the University of Notre Dame, has pointed out, this is actually an argument from self-interest.[12] Its logic is fairly straightforward: you should love all people and treat everyone with equal dignity because it will make your life better. The problem is that self-interest can only rationally support altruistic behavior for a limited number of people—those

73

people in close enough proximity to you that *their* well-being will positively impact *your* life.

When times get tough or hostile, or when we feel pressured to compete for limited resources, seeking the well-being of others may have an adverse effect on you and those closest to you. Truly living out universal benevolence is often difficult and painful. To support this aspiration we need a rationale that rises above the logic of self-interest.

Simply asserting, "But everyone I know intuitively knows these are good ideals," will not do. As we've seen, history tells a different story. In times of hardship and unrest, a clear moral logic is needed in order both to ground these high-level moral convictions and to persuade others to act with love and recognize the equal dignity of all. The historian Tom Holland makes the point that after World War II ended and the horrendous atrocities committed by the Nazis were revealed to the public, the main moral reference point in the popular imagination became, Don't be a Nazi![13] If a script writer needed bad guys for a movie, it was low-hanging fruit to simply introduce them as Nazis, or at least to have the actors dress and march like Nazis. (Keep this in mind the next time you watch *Star Wars*.) But as World War II fades from our collective memory and certain people begin to chant, "Blood, soil, and country," what resources do we have for creating a response? To brace ourselves in resistance to the cultural storms emerging on the horizon, we will need a clear moral logic grounded in something beyond sentiment and personal preferences.

Beyond just a clear moral logic, it is important to note the vast difference between holding high moral ideals and actually carrying on the work of caring for the impoverished and the neglected. A vague sense of what is sacred cannot provide the necessary motivation to be endlessly sacrificial and moral. Giving selflessly of one's money, time, health, social standing—even one's life—for the good of others is not easy. Why should I give of myself for others' sakes? Why suffer for people who cannot help me? How do I convince others that sacrificing for others is good? Does my spirituality provide a hope that will carry me through moments of despair? When it's all over, will justice and love have mattered at all?

To reach and sustain the standards set by our deepest aspirations of universal love and human dignity, we need more than a moral grounding; we need sources of moral motivation that are much stronger than mere sentiment. For true acts of love are costly. In order to flourish together, not with displays of superficial moral signaling but with love that is willing to suffer for the stranger or for those we don't like, we need a concrete story that justifies the high costs of such convictions. We need a collective script that undergirds our deepest moral aspirations.

A few years ago British atheist John Gray was on a podcast with a former pastor who had deconverted. Though the former pastor had given up on God, he still aspired to find a rationale, beyond personal sentiment, for moral ideals like the ones we've been discussing. The conversation was full of interesting details, but one moment surprised us. The former pastor asked Gray why secular people couldn't take certain sacred convictions with them into their post-Christian secular life. Gray explained that humans latch onto myths—stories that map meaning and shape people's experience. Secular attempts to hold sacred values rely on a tacit communal myth. But, he said, "they are shallower" than traditional religious myths, are "repeatedly falsified," and are "short-lived." Then he offered some advice: "If you want a myth beyond a personal myth, you are better off with the traditional religious myths."[14] For history has taught us which myths have proven more stable. As we turn to the final chapter of part 2, we will explore our final residence outside the Christian house, where people are trying out Gray's advice.

9

Mythic Truth

IN THE PREVIOUS CHAPTER, we introduced you to Rhett McLaughlin as a representative of open spirituality. We begin this chapter by stepping inside the world of Jordan Peterson, the evolutionary psychologist who represents the "mythic truth" approach to Christianity. These two thinkers are similar in that they both affirm many of the ethical stances of Jesus while remaining unconvinced of the veracity of Christianity's historical claims. However, their stories move in opposite directions. Rhett grew up as a Christian and has seen his recent journey lead away from the church; Peterson has grown more enamored with the Christian story over the past decade. Rhett has shifted toward more politically liberal stances while Peterson is, on many issues, seen as a champion of right-wing politics.

Peterson, like Rhett, sees Christianity as a "myth." But what is a myth? And why do myths matter? On this question the difference between Peterson and Rhett is pronounced. For Peterson, a myth is more than just an imaginative story that has been handed down over generations; myths provide and express life's meaning. Peterson is a controversial figure in modern sociopolitical discussions, but his political stances are not necessary to the mythic-truth stance. For example, Tom Holland, a secular liberal historian, also looks to the Christian myth for meaning and affirms that myths can be true.[1] However, we are exploring this space through the lens of Peterson because of his cultural influence as well as the confusion over how his views relate to Christianity.

The Myth of Meaning

When Fredrich Nietzsche famously declared that God was dead, his statement identified what was becoming a massive vacuum of meaning in human life. For those who accepted this secular turn, God was no longer *the* source of meaning. Many Enlightenment philosophers had considered rationality the most important feature of humanity. Nietzsche, seeing the vacuum, argued that the human capacity to make meaning was most central.[2] We all need meaning, and if meaning doesn't exist, then we have to make it. This is where Jungian psychology comes into play. Carl Jung, developing Nietzsche's ideas, suggested that our path to meaning could be found through the symbols, myths, and stories that communally shape our cultures. For Jung, these myths represented our collective unconscious.[3] Running counter to Nietzsche, Jung saw Christ as the "ideal hero."[4] The story of Christ's death and resurrection gives people hope and life in a profound way, and the story's power has little to do with its historicity. Instead, said Jung, the story is significant because it produces meaning in people's lives.

Peterson, following Jung, homes in on the human need to develop meaning in life. This is the central task of Peterson's books. To young people floundering in life, Peterson challenges them to take responsibility for themselves and others. Why? Because responsibility is a direct path to meaning in life. The act of caring for others provides a mission and direction for those stuck in a malaise of purposelessness.

Meaning, for Peterson, is not accessible solely through rational processes; no amount of cause and effect can ever render either the cause or the effect meaningful in and of itself. A purely mechanistic view of the world results in a life where we do things simply because we do, with no deeper meaning to our actions. For this reason the twenty-first century is poorly equipped to give people the proper resources to sustain the belief and meaning they need. As Peterson puts it, "The individual cannot live without belief—without action and valuation—and science cannot provide that belief. We must nonetheless put our faith into something."[5]

"Faith" here doesn't mean what Christians might think. Peterson is not committed to all of Christianity's historical claims, but he does think the Christian story provides a meaning-producing myth for humanity. In fact, Peterson has said that many people who listen to his lectures could describe themselves as "Christian atheists."[6] These people don't believe in God—they reject the undergirding beliefs that hold Christian ethics in place—but Peterson's description of Christian ethics resonates with them. They love his lectures on Genesis and his teachings on responsibility. In many ways they want to live *as if* Christianity is real, and that is exactly what Peterson encourages them to do.

This commitment to living *as if* Christianity is true transcends simple ethical rules like "do to others what you would have them do to you" (Matt. 7:12). The commitment stretches all the way to how we imagine the world around us. Why should we treat others with compassion? Because it is moral to do so and our communal myth teaches us that all people are infused with dignity. At a deep, subconscious level, we know that people deserve to be treated with compassion. Peterson would tell you that your subconscious has imbibed this from the communal myths we share. This is where mythic truth starts separating itself from the open spirituality we explored in the previous chapter.

To live out Christian teachings—like living sacrificially and caring for others—we require subconscious faith commitments. Simply living rationally will not get anyone there. Peterson points out that fascism and communism in the twentieth century were "rational, logical, statable, comprehensible—and terribly wrong."[7] We must act in order to live, and when we act, we have to make choices and value things. But how can we know what to value if rationality alone can't get us there? Peterson explains, "It is, traditionally speaking, our knowledge of good and evil, our moral sensibility, that allows us this ability. It is our mythological conventions, operating implicitly or explicitly, that guide our choices."[8] A simple openness is not sufficient, in Peterson's view. We need commitment.

Peterson sees the rise of New Age spirituality in the West as evidence of the human tendency to focus on all the wrong problems.[9] He rightly observes that while New Age spirituality might give a vague sense of meaning and significance, that meaning is locked into private and unstable sentiments. But for Peterson, the problems of vague spirituality go beyond the individual. For without some sort of cohesive narrative to explain the meaning we are all searching for, we can't forge lasting societal peace.[10] As our spiritualities become atomized, so, too, will our sources of meaning. Meaning will become a purely individual metric and—in an ironic turn of events—lose its meaning entirely.

To consider the implications of this problem, consider where Nietzsche's reasoning led him. In his view Christianity was a blight holding humanity back, and the only way forward was to undo the Christian fixation with "eternal valuations."[11] Instead, he believed, humans should focus on what they could become, what they could achieve.[12] But for this to happen, Christianity would have to be overthrown; it was too fixated on the weakest members of society. By caring for the oppressed, the sick, the suffering, and the helpless, Christianity was working toward "the deterioration of the European race!"[13] This was being allowed, according to Nietzsche, only because "men, not sufficiently noble to see the radically different grades of rank and intervals of rank that separate man from man: —SUCH men, with their 'equality before God,' have hitherto swayed the destiny of Europe."[14]

Since Nietzsche saw meaning primarily through the advancement of humanity, he perceived anyone who was weak or helpless as a hindrance to that meaning. Since he saw smart and successful Europeans as the most important resource for achieving the advancement of humanity, he believed all other people should be viewed as less valuable.

If you instinctually recoil from these positions, it's because you have different values than Nietzsche did—to say the least. And as historians like Tom Holland and Kyle Harper have shown, it also means you have radically different values from the brutal ancient world in which Christianity was born.[15] And since you are reading this book in English, you probably have many of these sensibilities because you grew up in a culture shaped by the Christian myth. For instance, Jürgen Habermas, an important secular philosopher, has admitted that "there is no alternative to" the heritage of the "Judaic ethic of justice and the Christian ethic of love" as the basis for the ideals of "freedom and a collective life in solidarity, the autonomous conduct of life and emancipation, the individual morality of conscience, human rights and democracy."[16]

Our values rarely, if ever, come through direct choice but instead are inherited through the myths found in the bloodstream of culture and pumped into our veins through the stories, songs, symbols, and icons that fill our lives. By retelling and reimagining mythic accounts, cultures forge shared visions of morality that allow for peaceful coexistence.[17]

This is why Holland says that we, in some sense, need Christianity in order to maintain our moral commitments in the modern secular world. Even though he seems unsure about God's existence, he sees himself as a Christian when it comes to his values.

> There's a power to [Christianity]. This is the most powerful way of explaining what humans are about that has ever existed, in terms of its impact, its influence, the numbers who've followed it. And so I feel an incredible tug. You know, if I'm not just going to become a kind of Nietzschean, let's-revel-in-power! kind of nihilist, I have to take this leap of faith. And if I've got to take a leap of faith to believe this stuff that I viscerally believe in, I might as well hang for a sheep as a lamb.[18]

But can it work for people to affirm that Christianity is simply a useful "myth"? Is it reasonable to expect people to take a "leap of faith" into the ethics and morals of Christianity when they do not have a belief in its truth claims? Does our myth need to be historically true?

Plot Holes in This Mythic Story

To be fair, Peterson is particularly open about his own struggle, and he sometimes teeters between the mythic-truth approach and a real commitment to Christianity (including its historical claims). He says that "in the person of Christ you have an actual person who actually lived plus a myth, and in some sense . . . I probably believe that, but I am amazed at my own belief, and I don't understand it."[19] Yet he also says that Christianity's historical claims are "too terrifying a reality to fully believe." He doesn't "even know what would happen to you if you fully believed it."[20] This is because the Christian story, if true, means that "the narrative and the objective [worlds] can actually touch."[21]

Someone in the mythic-truth camp may conclude that it doesn't really matter whether Christianity's historical claims are true or not. After all, if you can live *as if* Christianity is true, does it matter if it really is? But for New Testament Christianity, the historical claims are central. If there is no God and no resurrection, we are no longer even talking about Christianity. Christianity works because it is true, not the other way around. If the claims of Christianity touch reality—if Jesus Christ really rose from the dead—it changes everything. If the historical claims of Christianity are real, we cannot just live *as if* Christianity were true. We need to realize that we live within the *true* myth.

In a Jungian frame the suffering we experience is a trial to overcome. Suffering can strengthen us. Adversity gives us the metaphorical weights for training ourselves and becoming more resilient. This is the metaphorical resurrection; suffering and defeat leads to resilience and growth. This mythic truth is deeply cemented into our minds, finding its way into our collective stories as a means to help us cope with this hard world—or so the Jungian account goes.

But what about those times when suffering doesn't seem to strengthen us? What happens when someone you love wounds you deeply and there's little hope for reconciliation? Or when your child dies unexpectedly? Or when you are diagnosed with cancer? What power does resurrection have in these times if it's *only* a myth? If people do not believe a myth is really true, the myth is useless for them when most needed. In other words, a myth is not enough for the human soul. Our internal compass is looking not just for something that works but also for a story that's really true.

But if you live in the myth believing that it is true, you will see the same teaching much differently. Yes, adversity and suffering can lead to growth. But no longer can the cold, hard realities of this world stunt or limit the myth's ultimate significance, for you will see the pattern of resurrection woven into the world around you. Summer's life may fade and die, but spring is around the corner. Death is not the end, for Jesus rose from the dead.

While death leading to resurrection is the most salient example, the power of living in the myth that is also a fact can be seen in other ways. Take, for example, love. Our lives revolve around story lines of love—love lost, love found, love at risk, and love leading to sacrifice. In the *Avengers: Endgame* movie, the moment when Tony Stark (Iron Man) snaps his fingers to save the world isn't powerful just because of the massive scope of his actions; it is powerful because his sacrificial love resonates with us.

The mythic-truth space tells us that humans value love, at least subconsciously. Its proponents might say Christianity is an ideal showcase for the centrality of love. But the mythic way falls short in justifying love and providing it with real substance. Is love important only because we think it is? Is love simply something that humans collectively want, a fleeting eccentricity of a momentary species? Can you justify to others, especially in a polarized society, that a love stretching beyond their particular tribe is good? If you cannot justify it to them—if they choose to be selfish, hateful, violent, or aggressive—how can your focus on love be more than a parochial sensibility, something you just happen to prefer? And if you admit that such morals are really only temporary preferences, will you be able to carry on with this way of life, knowing full well that these lofty ideals are relative? Human history suggests that for love to be substantive, powerful, and lasting, people need more than a mythic truth.

This leads to a final problem with Peterson's use of the Christian myth. He misunderstands one of the most important features of Christianity: the nature of divine love. While his emphases on responsibility, sacrifice, and bearing one's cross find a home in the Christian narrative, Jesus does not offer a gospel of responsibility and self-confidence. Instead, Christianity tells a story of divine love, punctuated by scandalous grace and forgiveness.[22]

Peterson is correct to a point: individuals and societies need a coherent story to live by. But if we skim over grace and the importance of Christianity's central historical claim, we are no longer talking about Christianity.

Christianity as the True Myth

Lewis himself was a proponent of a mythic way of knowing, albeit with some significant differences.[23] Lewis understood that Jesus's actual resurrection was essential to the power of the Christian story. A "Christian atheist" is a contradiction in terms. Lewis came to inhabit the Christian house because he believed it told the myth that was also a fact, the myth that had broken into history. Lewis came to see that Christianity represented the fulfillment of all human hope. It really is, as Peterson and Jung would see it, the ideal story about the ideal hero. But it is God's story fulfilled in the person of Jesus, marked by truth and grace. In that sense it is almost too perfect. The belief that all humans are loved by God and that Jesus gave himself up for each of us can seem, at times, too good to be true, the ultimate wish fulfillment. But if Christianity *is* true, it would make sense that his image bearers would be made to see it as the greatest of all stories—to wish for it. Of course, if it is true that something in the world and within our own hearts has gone wrong, as the Christian story says, it would also make sense that humanity would paradoxically desire and despise the story of a heavenly Father. We're like a teenage child, aching for the love of our father while also rebelling against his authority. We desire transcendent love and cosmic significance, but we seek them on our own terms.

We'll talk more about this paradox later, but for now, don't miss that Lewis's discovery didn't denigrate all other stories or religious myths as completely wrong. For if Lewis was right, what is "vaguely hinted in all the religions at their best . . . comes into focus in Christianity."[24] In this way Christianity is the climactic culmination of all our past mythic hopes, as vague and distorted as they were, because in them the ancients were grasping for the hope that would one day arrive in history through a real person, the "myth which is also a fact."[25]

Another Look at the House

The individuals we've referenced in this chapter know many of the pressures of mythic truth intimately. For example, while Tom Holland may have given up on Christian faith as a child, he has returned to the church.[26] He might not be a "full" believer, but he is no longer naive about the source of his moral aspirations. Holland recognizes that the deepest moral commitments of the Western world are rooted in Christianity, and his recognition of this fact leads him to wonder whether Christianity is, in fact, the true myth.

Recall that we started this part of the book by introducing you to Augustine, who, similar to Holland, left an attic full of doubts in order to try out other residences. After years of searching he found himself uncertain and unhappy but not yet ready to return to faith. But then he met a man who gave him reason to pause, a man who, despite his great importance, was, as Augustine put it, "kind to me." The man was the learned and eloquent preacher Ambrose. Purely out of professional interest, Augustine went to hear him speak. At first Augustine cared little for what Ambrose was saying. Then something started happening. Augustine realized, gradually, that he had run away from a caricature of Christianity. He came to see that believing was at least "intellectually respectable."[27] He soon began "doubting everything" but sensed that perpetual doubt could never be a final destination. Then Augustine, like Holland, decided to return to the church and take another look. This time, however, he approached Christianity with a different posture. We, having followed Augustine's approach in this part of the book by exploring different residences outside the Christian house, now turn to follow him back into the house and have another look around.

84

INTERLUDE

Before Exploring Downstairs

JUST AS AUGUSTINE WAS INTRODUCED by Ambrose to the main floor of Christianity, we, too, need guides to help us see what Christianity outside the attic is like. One of the reasons we've continued to look to C. S. Lewis is that as a professor of medieval literature, much of his thought life was directly connected to the ancient rooms of the Christian house.[1] This gave him a stable vantage point from which to see beyond his day's denominational battlelines and the tribal signaling of those who imagine their particular attic is the entire house. Lewis retrieved the main floor's treasures and, with them, presents a capacious and illuminating picture of the Christian faith. You might still reject this kind of Christianity in the end, but if you're willing to look *at* and *along*, as Lewis suggests, you will at least find a Christianity that cannot easily be rejected as shallow or naive.

Furthermore, as a former atheist and later as a widower, Lewis knew what it was like to wrestle with doubt both before and after faith. His struggles with doubt make him a model guide for living with questions in the Christian house. But there is another reason that we find him relevant. In Lewis we discover a way to be Christian that takes the pressures of disenchantment seriously while refusing to build an isolated attic rife with fear, inferiority complexes, and loathing. Before exploring the main floor in earnest, let's briefly examine Lewis's approach.

The Lewis Option

In 1943 Lewis published *The Abolition of Man*. In this short but dense work, Lewis argues that the Western world has begun to reject what every prior civilization has accepted as foundational: there is a grain to the universe that we should seek to discover and live within. Lewis critiques the "extreme rationalism" that, ironically, subjects individuals to the whims of their preferences.[2] The West has turned inward and elevated mere impulse. If this trajectory is carried forward, Lewis feared, it would lead to the abolition of humanity itself.

As you might have surmised from his dour title, Lewis isn't optimistic about the modern world. Like those in the attic, Lewis saw serious problems with movements afoot in the twentieth century, yet he saw the problems with a depth and clarity that sets him apart from those in today's attic. Still, Lewis didn't spend the rest of his career building an attic out of the scrap timber of anger and fear. While offering serious warnings, he presented the treasures found on the main floor of the Christian house, highlighting the importance of joy and desire and writing imaginative stories, many of them for children. Why? Because "Lewis was nostalgic for the future."[3]

Lewis recognized just how deep the modern world's malaise is, understanding that we have lost not just a moral code but also a way to see. As James Davison Hunter puts it, "The world has actually changed in deeper ways than what we can see and for reasons that are much more complicated than the rise in secularism. When people observe a weakening in public virtue or traditional personal character, they tend to blame the artifacts of change and not the sources of change."[4]

Those in the attic spend the bulk of their time responding to things that they don't like, including shifting public policies and moral sentiments. But too often they are not paying attention to the deeper sources behind these changes. The problem is not simply whatever might be the polarizing headline of the day. The problem is the way we intuitively imagine and attend to the world.

Lewis suggests that the way for us to see more of reality is to expand our imaginations and rediscover life's deepest pleasures. He often reminds readers that careful logic and thinking are vital. Yet he also understands that our thinking is always embedded in larger imaginative visions of the world. He saw that our inherited modern social constructs profoundly, and at times adversely, affect what we value and believe. But what can we do about that? Lewis believed it was the true and deep pleasures in life that could reorient us to reality. As Lewis puts it, what we need is "the scent of a flower we have not found, the echo of a tune we have not heard, news from a country we have never yet visited."[5] Then, anticipating that some listeners will reject this suggestion, he asks, "Do you think I am trying to weave a spell? Perhaps I am; but remember your fairy tales. Spells are used for breaking enchantments as well as for inducing them. And you and I have need of the strongest spell that can be found to wake us from the evil enchantment of worldliness which has been laid upon us for nearly a hundred years."[6]

Lewis is particularly sensitive to the fact that the disenchantment of the modern world impairs us from seeing what previous civilizations saw plainly. The modern world's sharp distinction between fact and value and its relegation of values to the status of personal preference have hollowed out core features of our humanity—including courage, sacrifice, delight, and love. As Alan Jacobs observes, according to Lewis this modern posture "makes the universe silent and vague, so we come to resemble it. It shrinks the scope of human action, mistrusting or debunking the heroic and the noble; we shrink correspondingly."[7]

Lewis does not naively imagine that the ancients had everything correct about science, or ethics, or politics. But he is persuaded that modern people, by believing their own press about having come of age, have lost much ancient wisdom. He looks back because he believes that our forebears are uniquely able to diagnose our underlying disorder. He looks backward not because he is pining for some kind of nostalgic golden age but rather because he wants to "move forward and look beyond."[8]

While our present world keeps giving us more information and better technology, it has also set new terms for how we attend to the world, such that it binds and blinds us and resets our posture so subtly that this new posture feels completely natural. Lewis asks us to consider whether or not it really is natural. On this point philosopher Mary Midgley has observed how machine imagery began to dominate in the seventeenth century:

> Where microscopes dominate our imagination, we feel that the large wholes we deal with in everyday experience are mere appearances. Only the particles revealed at the bottom of the microscope are real. Thus, to an extent unknown in earlier times, our dominant technology shapes our symbolism and thereby our metaphysics, our view about what is real.[9]

All of our inherited pictures and metaphors of the world are a socially constructed way of seeing that both opens us up to see new things and blinds us from other important realities. If God feels absent, or the gospel has stopped making sense, or the evidence that you used to find compelling now seems unconvincing, then on one level you do need to think carefully through each issue. But if Lewis is right, then on a deeper level you will need to examine your posture carefully. A thorough readjustment of your alignment might be necessary if you are to gain the vantage point by which you can see the bigger picture.

The final part of the book argues that the way through our disillusionment and paralyzing doubt is neither to fearfully shut ourselves up in an attic nor to desperately leap out the attic window. On the one hand, the attic's low-hanging rafters and the encroaching walls will leave us misaligned, perhaps even incapacitated, in the face of our doubts. On the other hand, jumping out of the window might turn out to be just as debilitating. Besides, a leap from the attic will mean avoiding the main floor—where Christianity is meant to be tried and tested. To discover if the Christian house is sturdy, we need to walk downstairs. The main floor not only offers a different perspective to see, it prescribes ways to rehabilitate our posture. On the main floor we will look closely *at* the claims of Jesus, but we won't simply look at him. We will also learn to stand up straight to look *through* him and step *into* his ways so we can see how his message illuminates the world and changes our experience in it.[10]

Part Three

———

THE MAIN FLOOR

Perspective 1
Looking At

Perspective 2
Looking Through

Perspective 3
Stepping In

10

The Historical Foundation

WHEN THE CATHOLIC NOVELIST Walker Percy was asked, "Why are you Catholic?" he would usually reply, with what we imagine was a wry smile, "What else is there?"[1]

In part 2 we explored "what else" is outside the Christian house. We ventured to some of the most popular spaces that those who leave the attic find themselves residing in.

Now, as we turn to explore the main floor of the Christian house, we're asking a different question: Does Christianity offer a better foundation, better explanatory power, and a better way to live than the spaces we explored in part 2?

When life gets hard, the wise person makes use of triage. Triaging is determining what is most important and then focusing on tasks that support it. ER nurses and doctors do this when patients arrive. If you have chest pains, you will receive treatment before the person with the cut on their hand. To give a lighter example, think of how triaging is wise when considering a home investment. A house might be renovated beautifully, but if there is reason to think the foundation is bad, you're wasting your time admiring the marble countertops. Countertops are an easy fix compared to the foundation.

In trying to navigate your doubts, have you focused primarily on Christianity's foundation or on certain unseemly additions? Have you focused on the bedrock claims of Christ or on questions that don't have to be—and perhaps will never be—answered in this life?

Triaging means coming back to what is essential. By all means leave the attic. But if you can believe Jesus rose from the dead, you have a good reason to stay in the house. We will come back to the differences between essentials and distinctives in chapter 12, but for this chapter and the next, we ask that you try to keep first things first. Make up your mind about whether Jesus is worth betting on, and then go from there.

Historical Markers

The historical points that scholars of all stripes have pretty much agreed on are a fitting place to begin. We're looking for common historical ground, so to speak, or what has been called "the minimal facts."[2]

First, Jesus died on a cross. Almost all scholars today, even those who are not Christians, agree that Jesus died by crucifixion. Why? Because numerous early Christian and non-Christian sources say so. Furthermore, it wouldn't have made sense for the early disciples to make this up. Matthew, Mark, Luke, and John all include awkward accounts of Jesus's own disciples misunderstanding or failing to believe Jesus when he told them, repeatedly, that he must die. The disciples' confusion makes historical sense: no first-century Jew was expecting the long-awaited Messiah to die by way of a killing device reserved for the most despised criminals. Nobody had "Israel's savior-king will be crucified" on their first-century bingo card. And yet the earliest sources agree that he was.

Second, Jesus's corpse was never produced. If his corpse had been discovered in or around Jerusalem, where Jesus died and where the resurrection story originated, the early Christian movement would have been undermined from the start. To deal with this upstart movement, the authorities would have had only to retrieve the corpse from the place of burial. For historians, the question is

94

not whether his corpse was produced but rather why it wasn't. We will return to possible explanations later.

Third, some of Jesus's earliest followers began to proclaim Jesus had risen from the dead. The earliest Christian creeds, oral traditions, and other early historical writings all underscore that the resurrection was foundational to early Christian belief. Why is there such widespread acceptance of the historicity of this point? Because there is no viable explanation for the historical rise of Christianity without its earliest adherents proclaiming that Jesus rose again.

The Best Explanation?

If you grant these three historical facts—Jesus died on a cross, his body was never produced, and his earliest disciples proclaimed he rose from the dead—the question is not what can be proven, since that is not how such historical questions are answered, but what the best explanation is.

The Greeks detested the idea of a resurrected body. They had a dualistic worldview in which the soul was spiritual and good but the physical body was temporary and unwanted. Hence, the claim that Jesus rose from the dead—body and all—would have been a nonstarter. For first-century Jews, Jesus's bodily resurrection wouldn't have been detestable, but it would have seemed implausible. While some Jews at this time did look forward to the resurrection of the dead, they placed their hopes in a future corporate resurrection that would accompany the transformation of all creation, not the bodily resurrection of one man in the middle of time in a world plagued by unrest, enmity, and sin. No one was expecting the Messiah, after a shameful death on a cross, to rise from the dead. If the early disciples were trying to use a false claim to get traction for their cause, this wouldn't have been it.[3]

In fact, we know from the historical record that Jesus was not the first would-be messiah to garner a following before being executed. Historians have cataloged at least a dozen other messianic movements from around this time.[4] Yet none of these movements' followers ever claimed their leader was resurrected. New Testament scholar N. T. Wright explains why:

> In not one single case do we hear the slightest mention of the disappointed followers claiming that their hero had been raised from the dead. They knew better. "Resurrection" was not a private event. It involved human bodies. There would have to be an empty tomb somewhere. A Jewish revolutionary whose leader had been executed by the authorities, and who managed to escape arrest himself, had two options: give up the revolution or find another leader. . . . Claiming that the original leader was alive again was simply not an option.[5]

In other words, it is historically implausible to think Jesus's disciples would have made up an event that no one was expecting—namely, the resurrection. There must really have been some kind of remarkable event causing them to make such a claim.

There are two more things worth mentioning that challenge the idea that these earliest disciples simply made it all up. For one, it is unlikely they would have chosen women to be the first eyewitnesses to circulate the story. Authorities at this time did not consider women credible witnesses, so using women's testimonies to support the outlandish claim of resurrection would have been the height of folly for anyone seeking to deceive the public. Given that women are, in fact, the first eyewitnesses in all the Gospel traditions, it is very likely that the Gospel writers were committed to telling what they believed actually happened, awkward details and all.[6]

Second, the idea that the disciples simply made up the resurrection fails to explain their transformation. In order to give a credible historical explanation for the origins of the Christian house, we need to be able to account for how the earliest disciples so quickly moved from lamenting their leader's death and the failure of their mission to risking their lives for the sake of proclaiming Jesus's resurrection to the very same people who had crucified Jesus. It is difficult to imagine why, if it were all an enormous ruse, just one big lie, they would have taken it so far and for so long.[7]

All these reasons confirm that the earliest Christians believed that Jesus bodily rose from the grave. Bart Ehrman agrees: "It is indisputable that some of the followers of Jesus came to think that he had been raised from the dead, and something had to have happened to make them think so."[8] More interesting is that Ehrman, while not believing in the resurrection, does accept all three of our basic historical points. He concludes that Jesus's early disciples genuinely believed in a resurrection that *did not happen*.

But how could these disciples be convinced they had seen Jesus alive and yet be sincerely wrong? Ehrman offers this in response: "Some of Jesus' followers had visions of him alive after he had been crucified."[9] By "visions" he is not implying that Jesus actually appeared after his death, and he admits that psychologists today would likely call these "visions" hallucinations.[10] Is the vision/hallucination theory the best explanation? For several reasons, we don't think so.

First, bereavement and esteemed-figure hallucinations do not adequately explain the multiple, diverse claims about disciples seeing Jesus after his death. In 1 Corinthians 15:3–7, for instance, Paul cites creedal material that likely originated just a few years after Jesus's death. Paul claims that Jesus appeared to Peter, then to the twelve disciples, then to more than five hundred people, then to James (Jesus's half brother), then to the apostles—and that many of these witnesses were still alive at the time of his writing. In other words, Paul is inviting accountability. These witnesses could be found and questioned. This early creedal material can be combined with the variety of reports throughout the New Testament, which Peter Williams lists concisely:

> The resurrected Jesus is recorded as appearing in Judaea and in Galilee, in town and countryside, indoors and outdoors, in the morning and in the evening, by prior appointment and without prior appointment, close and distant, on a hill and by a lake, to groups of men and groups of women, to individuals and groups of up to five hundred, sitting, standing, walking, eating, *always* talking. Many are explicitly close-up encounters involving conversations. It is hard to imagine

this pattern of appearances in the Gospels and early Christian letters without there having been multiple individuals who claimed to have seen Jesus risen from the dead.[11]

The hallucination theory accepts that his followers actually saw something, which seems to us a better explanation than the theory that suggests the disciples simply made it up. But those who accept the hallucination theory as well as the historical witnesses in 1 Corinthians 15, or even just a few of the reports found in the Gospels, must admit these visions occurred with both individuals and groups and with remarkably consistent depictions of Jesus. The hallucination explanation also raises other challenging questions. Given that people in the ancient world knew what hallucinations were, why would they conclude that Jesus had risen from the dead when they weren't expecting a resurrection in the first place? If they were hallucinating, why was that not the explanation? Or if they knew people had visions, why not claim that Jesus had assumed some kind of exalted status? For as we've seen, resurrection was a counterintuitive claim that would not have readily come to mind. Why up the ante by claiming there was a resurrected physical body?

Even if someone were willing to accept all of the elements of this theory so far, it doesn't explain why Paul also saw a vision of Jesus. Before his conversion Paul was not grieving Jesus's death. In fact, Paul persecuted Christians. Yet he repeatedly states that Jesus appeared and spoke to him. This testimony requires that a separate theory, proposing a unique psychological state for Paul, be added to the hallucination theory in order to explain the evidence.

Second, this theory struggles to explain the missing corpse. Ehrman, for instance, claims that the Romans wouldn't have allowed Jesus to be given a proper burial and that his body was therefore likely eaten by animals or simply discarded. If Jesus's crucifixion occurred during wartime, this would have more historical merit. Let's test this theory and imagine that not giving a proper burial was the known practice in and around Jerusalem in peacetime during the time of Jesus's death. A question immediately arises: If this were the case, why did those who objected to the Christian claims not offer a simple and obvious reply to the proclamation of resurrection: "Everyone knows the body of Jesus wasn't buried, because that was not allowed"? If not burying bodies was a common practice in Jerusalem during this time, as Ehrman argues, this would be the straightforward response. But no one that we are aware of offered such a reply. Instead, the response offered by early critics was that the body was stolen.[12]

This response fits with what we know from other historical witnesses. As the historian Craig Evans has shown, the normal Roman practice was to allow for Jewish burial practices in and around Jerusalem:

> The Jewish historian and Apologist [Josephus] adds that the Roman procurators who succeeded Agrippa I "by abstaining from interface with the customs of the country kept the nation at peace" (*Jewish War* 2.220), customs that included never leaving a "corpse unburied" (*Against Apion* 2.211). Had Roman governors—in Israel, especially in the vicinity of Jerusalem itself—regularly crucified Jews and left their bodies hanging on crosses, it is unlikely they would have "kept the nation at peace."[13]

Moreover, according to the Jewish scholar Jodi Magness, the best archaeological evidence suggests that the

> Gospel accounts of Jesus' burial are largely consistent with the archeological evidence. Although archeology does not prove there was a follower of Jesus named Arimathea or that Pontius Pilate granted his request for Jesus' body, the Gospel account describing Jesus' removal from the cross and burial are consistent with archeological evidence and Jewish law.[14]

If, due to the strong historical evidence, you accept these three minimal facts recognized by the vast majority of scholars, you are left with a couple of choices. You could bet on some alternative explanation that denies Jesus's resurrection. However, the hallucination/vision explanation is probably as good as you'll find, and as we've seen, it has some serious challenges. Or you could, as we have done, bet on the resurrection. Wagering on the resurrection doesn't mean that all your questions will be answered or that you have absolute certainty. It does mean, however, that even while you might still live with nagging questions and doubts, there are historical reasons to believe.

Wait a Minute

But at this point you might find yourself objecting, "Wait just a minute. I will admit that some scholars might be making a stronger case for the resurrection than the one I heard growing up, but isn't it better to say that we don't really know what happened? Why commit to saying a dead man actually rose from the dead?"

Imagine that a group of people came by your house tonight claiming to be witnesses to a man who rose back to life and would never die again. You'd probably shut the door as quick as you could and get back to whatever you were doing. You might not even consider an explanation necessary, for everybody knows that a dead person coming back to life is so implausible that you don't need to waste your time looking into it. Just shut the door. Walk away. Get back to tending your garden or watching the ballgame.

How is the claim of Jesus's resurrection any different?

The Christian claim is not that a random person rose from the dead, but that God, in fulfillment of the story of Israel, became human and, in an act of supreme love for the world, died—and then was resurrected. That is a shocking claim. Maybe in the end it is too much for you to believe. Yet it is not the same as our hypothetical situation above. This is no random Joe coming back to life.

More directly to the issue, we need to avoid the notion that people in the first century were naive about how the world works. They didn't go around readily believing that dead people were resurrected. As we've discussed, it seems to have taken a pattern of miraculous events for Jesus's followers to believe it had really happened. Even Augustine, more than three hundred years later, was in awe over the far-reaching acceptance of Jesus's resurrection:

Now we have three incredible things, and yet all three have actually happened. It is incredible that Christ rose in the flesh and ascended with his flesh into heaven. It is incredible that the world has come to believe something so incredible. It is incredible that a few obscure men, of no standing and with no education, were able to be so effective in persuading the world, including even the learned, of something so incredible.[15]

Augustine goes on to explain that the last two historical facts cannot be denied. For those in his time who insisted on denying the first point, the resurrection, Augustine writes that it "still leave[s] us with this one great miracle—that the whole world has come to believe it without any miracles at all."[16] In other words, the idea that people all throughout the world have been believing in a miracle—for two thousand years now—without an actual miracle having taken place would be a "miracle" in and of itself. To go back to our hypothetical story, what if it wasn't a random small group of people claiming a resurrection but, instead, multitudes of people throughout your city, your country, and the entire world? Surely then it would merit turning off the ballgame or pulling off the gardening gloves to give the claim some serious attention.

Still, something has changed since Augustine's time, beyond just the multiplication of Christians throughout the world. Today, as we have seen, many of us live in Western subcultures that shape our imaginations so that we assume a disenchanted universe and thus have more difficulty accepting miracles. Yet to the extent that this is the case, this development speaks more to our limited experiences and plausibility structures than to the actual rationality of miraculous claims. Most of the world still takes for granted that miracles happen.

The historian Craig Keener has documented, in two volumes, thousands of credible claims of miracles, with multiple witnesses offering corroborating reports.[17] For anyone who is thinking of rejecting the resurrection as implausible, Keener's two volumes are worth examining. Or consider the case studies in the recent shorter book by the Princeton scholar Dale Allison, *Encountering*

Mystery.[18] For even if just one of the reports from Keener or Allison is a true miracle or encounter, then it would refute the notion of a closed, material-only universe. Plus, as we've discussed in chapter 6, there are good reasons not to assume a purely naturalistic material universe. Given each of our limited experiences, the intellectually open-minded approach is to refrain from ignoring the possibility of miracles.

In this chapter we have seen historical reasons for wagering on the resurrection. Not "proof," not rationally coercive evidence, but strong historical reasons for believing in the resurrection. To think more about this wager, the next thing to do is to take a fresh look *at* Jesus himself. Perhaps now, outside the confines of the attic, looking at Jesus will remind you why Christianity might just be worth wagering on.

11

The Person at the Center

NO PERSON IN HUMAN HISTORY has commanded a breadth of attention equal to that commanded by Jesus of Nazareth. It should not surprise us, then, that we often lose track of Jesus in the midst of all the different ways his life is leveraged for competing agendas. Even in our late-modern age, Christianity possesses immense cultural and political energy. Yet Christianity began as a movement centered on a particular person, not as an abstract set of deductions and certainly not as a policy solution to modern political problems.

Our thoughts about Jesus are often colored by the people who introduced us to him, and if you grew up in the attic, your image of Christ has been shaped by the particular concerns of that room. If you've grown cynical through the years because of the failings in your religious community—perhaps the abuse scandals or financial self-dealing that seem depressingly common—it can be easy to view Jesus through that lens. To respond with disappointment, and even anger, to hypocritical corruption is right. But disillusionment with attic Christianity doesn't have to leave you with a jaundiced view of Jesus; rather, it presents an opportunity to recalibrate around the person at the center of the faith.

What Can We Know?

The idea has taken root in some people's minds that the Jesus of the Gospels is more fable than fact. The real Jesus must have been different. Maybe the early Christians were just spinning tales and folklore that were embellished over time.

Historians over the past several decades have scrutinized this line of thought. Leading the way has been Richard Bauckham, a senior scholar at Cambridge University. Bauckham has spent a great deal of time examining the nature of the Gospels as eyewitness accounts.[1] An eyewitness does not have to be trusted, but their account should not be dismissed without examination. After all, when it comes to any ancient historical event or person, the only way we know anything is through human testimony. We don't have the space to trace these arguments, but if you're hung up on this issue, start with Bauckham's *Jesus: A Short Introduction* (or if you are more ambitious, get his much larger work, *Jesus and the Eyewitnesses*) or Peter Williams's *Can We Trust the Gospels?* These authors don't argue that everything in the Gospels can be proven to be true. As we saw in the previous chapter, that is not how history works. Instead, they make strong cases that the traditional four Gospels rely on eyewitness testimony and, as such, should be taken seriously as credible historical sources.

What Kind of Man Was Jesus?

We know that after Jesus's execution, a movement of followers claimed he was still alive. We also know that the religious leaders of his day—particularly Paul—began persecuting those followers within about a year of Jesus's death.[2] These varied and intense responses to Jesus's death arose in part from the claim that Jesus was, in some sense, God.[3] This claim surfaced in a Jewish environment that was strictly committed to monotheism. Expressing a belief that any human—no matter how great—was God amounted to blasphemy in the eyes of the religious leaders of that day (see, e.g., Mark 14:53–65).

We know from many different historical sources that the "veneration of Jesus" began "amazingly early."[4] For example, the apostle Paul wrote letters around AD 50 assuming that the worship of Jesus was already widely accepted in Christian circles. This suggests that people had begun worshiping Jesus within the first two decades after his death. Paul did not feel the need to defend the veneration of Christ; it was an assumed fact among the Christians to whom he wrote. The historian Larry Hurtado has shown in detail that "devotion to Jesus as divine erupted suddenly and quickly, not gradually and late, among first-century circles of followers. . . . Amid the diversity of earliest Christianity, belief in Jesus' divine status was amazingly common."[5]

What would it take for you to be convinced that one of your friends was God, the maker of heaven and earth, the source of life, and the redeemer of humanity? For us, and perhaps even more so for first-century Jews, the idea of worshiping a friend after he or she dies is preposterous. But Jesus's friends and early followers did exactly that.

Soon after his death Jesus's followers had experiences leading them to believe that he had been released from death, been given a glorious new body, received an exalted heavenly status, and commissioned them to proclaim his resurrection to the world.[6] Some of the earliest people to believe these things were Jesus's closest companions.

What kind of person lives a life that makes a claim to divinity seem remotely believable to those who, because of their convictions about God, are prone to be the most skeptical? What kind of person could be worshiped by his friends after traveling with them for years? (We have no doubt that if anyone went on a three-year hike with one of us, they'd be much more likely to want to kill us than worship us!) Even if you were to choose an option we looked at in the previous chapter and claim that Jesus's followers were hallucinating, the question still applies: What kind of person makes such an impression that his monotheistic followers come to believe he is God?

A Different Kind of Kingdom

In the Gospels Jesus often says shocking things. At a time when many of his followers are abandoning him, Jesus turns and asks his most loyal followers, "You do not want to leave too, do you?" Peter, a leader among those closest to Jesus, replies, "Lord, to whom shall we go? You have the words of eternal life. We have come to believe and to know that you are the Holy One of God" (John 6:67–69). How did Peter become convinced that Jesus was the "Holy One of God"? Why did Peter describe the teachings of Jesus as "the words of eternal life"? Or to use Jesus's favorite expression, what was so striking about his portrayal of the "kingdom of God" that his earliest followers bet their lives on him?

Jesus Models the Way of God's Kingdom

Most of us today take for granted that ethnic differences should not divide us. This was not the case in Jesus's world. Ethnic and gender divides were deeply ingrained in first-century Palestine. There were clearly established social hierarchies, and those at the top did not associate with those at the bottom. This custom was even stronger in the Jewish context, where traditions like purity laws could give social interactions a worrisome edge.

This is what makes Jesus's interactions with women and members of disenfranchised groups so compelling. In John 4, Jesus encounters a Samaritan woman at a public well. This woman is almost certainly a pariah; she is visiting the well during the hottest part of the day, a time when most members of the town would have avoided the chore. Her status as a social outcast has likely arisen from her marital history. She has been married five times and is now living with someone who is not her husband. People would consider this woman impure and immoral, the kind of woman that reputable people avoid. Among the religious elite of the time, it would have been unthinkable for a rabbi like Jesus to spend time with her. The author of the passage even writes that "Jews do not associate with Samaritans" (John 4:9). Jesus, however, speaks to this woman and asks her to share her water with him. Instead of treating her with scorn, Jesus upholds her dignity.

This surprises his disciples. Even those who have been spending time with him are still embedded within a social world that demands strict adherence to standards of propriety, regardless of the implications of those standards for the disenfranchised and downtrodden. But Jesus goes through his ministry with an open disregard for the social expectations of his world. He raises the moral bar of his day by establishing a new ethic. While the prevailing ethic of the day taught people to love their neighbor, the definition of "neighbor" was often flighty and obscure. Surely Samaritans are not the neighbors of the Jews.

In Luke 10 we find someone interacting with Jesus over this exact question. Responding to Jesus's admonition to love one's neighbor, a religious leader attempting to justify his lack of love responds by asking Jesus, "And who is my neighbor?" (v. 29). Jesus responds with the parable of the good Samaritan (vv. 30–37). In this parable he contrasts the kind actions of a Samaritan man against the uncaring actions of two religious leaders. Through this story Jesus challenges the biased and broken ethic that has caused the religious leader to look down on Samaritans.

Jesus lives the kind of life that challenges those around him to love more freely and more fully. He challenges discrimination and affirms the dignity of women. Meanwhile, some of the religious leaders of his day, much like people in our modern-day attic, have a fierce desire to build layers of protection against the impurities of the world. This fear-induced attitude leads them to neglect the very people that they should be caring for: their neighbors. Jesus boldly stands up to the powerful people of his day and serves the outcasts and the disenfranchised. He spends time with those who are deemed unclean by other rabbis and teachers, and his insistence on loving all people continuously puts him at odds with the prevailing authorities. Jesus's teachings pick up the moral trajectory set by the Hebrew Scriptures and start a universal revolution—one that has reverberated through history to our own day—of caring for the downtrodden and upholding the dignity of all people.

Jesus Turns the Tables on "Greatness" from within God's Kingdom

Jesus modeled strength *and* gentleness throughout his ministry, often in perplexing ways. While healing the sick, he refused earthly power and yet claimed the authority to forgive sins, leaving those who heard him scoffing, "He's blaspheming! Who can forgive sins but God alone?" (Mark 2:7). This combination was disorienting and—at least in the eyes of the religious leaders—dangerous.

Jesus was respected by a significant portion of his community. If he had wanted to he could have leveraged that influence to get himself into some position of power within the community. The Gospels suggest—and it makes perfect historical sense—that some of his followers were willing to revolt against the Romans and establish a new kingdom with Jesus as its ruler. Jesus tells them no. He shuns coercive force and lives a life of self-giving instead. His message is clear: one day he will be vindicated, but this future glory will come only by way of his sacrificial death.

When Jesus is on trial before his crucifixion, Caiaphas, the high priest, asks Jesus if he is the Son of God (Matt. 26:63). Jesus responds, "You have said so. . . . But I say to all of you: From now on you will see the Son of Man sitting at the right hand of the Mighty One and coming on the clouds of heaven" (v. 64). The high priest understands the outrageous nature of this claim and considers it blasphemy (v. 65).

If a friend of ours made a similar claim, we would assume they suffered from serious delusions of grandeur. But with Jesus, megalomania just doesn't fit.[7] Jesus is presented in the Gospels as simultaneously authoritative and gentle. Jesus does not use his power to take advantage; he does not seek out the rich and influential in order to enhance his own life. Rather, Jesus invites all "who are weary and burdened" to follow him, and he promises to give them rest. "Take my yoke upon you and learn from me, for I am gentle and humble in heart, and you will find rest for your souls" (Matt. 11:28–29). Greatness in our world is measured by the accumulation of power and the wielding of that power for one's own ends, but

Jesus models a different way. Yes, he promises he will come again in power to judge evil, but his power is seen also in his meekness. With his life and death, he left for us the model of true greatness: "The Son of Man did not come to be served, but to serve, and to give his life as a ransom for many" (Mark 10:45).

If you have encountered selfishness or corruption within the church, these things don't reflect the person at the center of the Christian house. The individuals who accumulate power at the expense of others are the same kind of people that Jesus challenged repeatedly throughout his ministry. Wielding power and wealth for selfish ends means acting contrary to the Christian message. The kind of life that Jesus invites us into is one of self-giving, not self-serving.

Jesus Scandalizes with the Grace of God's Kingdom

Jesus was, to say the least, controversial. He spoke with authority, challenged the pride of religious leaders, and turned his world's assumptions upside down. In Luke 15 we see religious leaders getting frustrated, complaining that Jesus "welcomes sinners and eats with them" (v. 2). In their minds it was the duty of rabbis and religious leaders to remain separated from society's sinners.

Jesus responds to their muttering with a story. In the parable of the prodigal son (Luke 15:11–32), a young man demands his inheritance from his father and proceeds to squander it all in a faraway country. The young son begins to starve and even resorts to eating out of a pig's trough, and when he finally decides to return home, he expects to be treated with scorn. After all, he had dishonored his father on two counts: first by demanding his inheritance and then by wasting it all. When he arrives home, he acknowledges to his father that he is no longer worthy to be called his son. The religious leaders of the day would have agreed: a son who disrespects his father so greatly doesn't deserve to be called a son.

But Jesus's parable takes a different turn. The father, seeing his son in the distance, races out to meet him with a loving embrace. He clothes him in the best robe, ring, and sandals he can find. He even throws a party in honor of his son's return: "For this son of mine was dead and is alive again; he was lost and is found" (Luke 15:24). This is what grace looks like.

The older son, however, is angered by the unmerited favor shown to his wayward brother. He was so irresponsible with their father's gifts. Why should he receive love and compassion? Bitter, the older brother leaves the party. He is a picture of the worst kind of tit-for-tat religion. And the religious leaders knew that Jesus was talking to them. Smug with their own self-righteousness and convinced of the merits of their outward purity, their hearts had become cold. They were like the older brother, refusing to celebrate the safe return of someone they ought to have loved. Yet there is still the offer of grace for the older brother, for the father goes to him and invites him to join the celebration.

Jesus's message of radical grace is too often domesticated. For example, as we saw in chapter 9, Jordan Peterson sees the core message of the cross as "Pick up your . . . damn cross and walk up the hill."[8] In other words, bear your suffering, even if it is unjust, and be transformed by taking responsibility for your life. This misses the fundamental message of Christ: namely, grace. The older brother's "gospel of responsibility" kept him from coming to the father. Likewise, the religious leaders' insistence on their own righteousness kept them from receiving Jesus. The scandalous good news Jesus offered in the first century is equally scandalous in our meritocracy: the Father is waiting to run out and embrace us, not because any of us have earned it but because of his unmerited love.

Believing That God Became Flesh

We are now in a better position to return to our opening question: How did such a dramatic shift happen that Jesus's earliest followers, strict monotheists, began worshiping him? The belief that Jesus rose from the dead was surely part of it, but there must have been more. His genius, his ethical teachings, his own exalted claims, and the overall shape of his life must have left such shocking, crater-sized impressions on his followers' memories that they began to imagine that Jesus might be more than a mere person. The four Gospels reflect a life that would have had that kind of impact.

In the accounts of the days leading up to Jesus's death, we read of his anguish, which reminds us of the both-and nature of Jesus that the church has long confessed. With driving authority he often spoke about a future judgment. Yet before the crucifixion he prayed in the garden, "Father, if you are willing, take this cup from me; yet not my will, but yours be done" (Luke 22:42). This side of Jesus's resurrection, it's easy to gloss over the pain and suffering that he experienced during his ministry and particularly in the days preceding his death. Doing so, however, undercuts one of the most significant things that Jesus modeled for us in this account: his humanity.

Yet even with the all-too-human temptation to save himself, Jesus laid down his life for others. He died for all, the haves and the have-nots—those who loved him and those who spat in his face. In his sacrifice we find what love and true greatness look like. Jesus prayed for those who crucified him, those who should have been his enemies: "Father, forgive them, for they do not know what they are doing" (Luke 23:34). But right after Jesus prayed, Luke tells us that "they divided up his clothes by casting lots" (v. 34). The injustice of the moment screams, but the act of forgiveness cries louder. Even at the very end of his life, Jesus was turning the tables. The just dying for the unjust. The guiltless taking on our guilt. Evil defeated by good. The King laying down his life for the kingdom.

We could never believe that any of our loved ones were, in some sense, God. We know too much about them—their sins and shortcomings. But in Jesus's case, quite shockingly, people who were closest to him began to believe he was somehow God himself. The Gospels remind us of the truth, beauty, and goodness of the life that invited worship from the earliest disciples—and has been doing so ever since.

12

The Load-Bearing Walls

IN THE MIDDLE OF THE GOSPEL OF MATTHEW, Jesus promises his disciples, "I will build my church, and the gates of hell shall not prevail against it" (16:18 ESV). At the end of the Gospel, Jesus reassures them he will be with them as they take his message to all nations (28:19–20). The average first-century person overhearing this would have assumed it to be a pipedream. When Matthew recorded those words, Christianity was not a major player on the world stage. Religious sects came and went. Of the small number of people who had heard of Christianity, most would never have imagined that this sect, propagating a counterintuitive message of a crucified King, would make a blip on history's radar. So, with a little historical imagination, we can see why an ancient Roman citizen, hearing these words from Matthew's Gospel, might have chuckled with skeptical amusement.

And yet here we are. Rarely do such bold predictions turn out to be true—with two thousand years of supporting data.

Currently, over two billion people in the world practice some form of Christianity, about one-third of the global population. The list of the ten countries with the most Christians is impressive in its diversity: United States, Brazil, Mexico, Nigeria, Philippines, Russia, Democratic Republic of Congo, Italy, Ethiopia, and China.[1]

One of the features contributing to the remarkable fulfillment of these predictions has been Christianity's *stable flexibility*. It is *stable* in that the basic elements of the Christian story have united Christian communities through time and space: a God who created and sustains the universe, humans who are made in his image but marred by sin, the God who became human, the crucified and risen Savior, hope in a future resurrection of the dead. Wherever there are Christians, we find these beliefs.

Yet Christianity has also displayed *flexibility*. Christianity's DNA is such that it can enter the bloodstream of a culture without desecrating its history and cultural expressions. In a departure from other major religions, no Christian monoculture exists. In fact, as the missiologist Andrews Walls has observed, one of the unique aspects of Christianity is that its geographical center migrates.[2] While Christians have rightly insisted that every culture should be examined carefully, its false gods and evil practices being critiqued, Christians have long understood that as history unfolds and as Christianity migrates to new places, fresh insights and beauty will be discovered.[3] This is akin to the famous Augustinian phrase "plundering the Egyptians."[4] Truth, wherever we find it, is God's truth.

We open this chapter with these observations because the walls of the attic sometimes obscure Christianity's surprising and remarkable history. This stifles our ability to learn from the deep unity and rich diversity of Christianity's past and present.

Finding the Load-Bearing Walls

This brings us to the load-bearing walls of the Christian faith.[5] Attic Christianity mistakenly makes the house appear as though most of its walls are load-bearing or at least integrally attached to the load-bearing walls. But then how do we know which walls are essential to the structure of the house? How do we go about discerning between the load-bearing walls of the house and the walls of a particular room? The answer is to step back and see how the whole house was built.

We have already seen the origins of Christianity in the person of Jesus and his resurrection. From the beginning Jesus and his followers sought to live in accordance with the Hebrew Scriptures. After Jesus's death his followers looked to both these ancient Scriptures and Jesus's teachings as their primary authorities. Following the resurrection, Jesus's first disciples took on leadership roles, teaching through their travels, proclamations, and letters. As the church continued to spread, new Christians repeated the apostolic messages in their communities by copying and passing around their writings. The writings came to be called Scripture and were afforded a status on par with the Hebrew Scriptures. They weren't yet part of an officially sanctioned list, but from a very early point the church recognized them to be "authoritative, sacred, and authentic."[6]

This brief sketch leads us to the answer of how the early Christians identified the faith's load-bearing walls. The New Testament scholar Michael Bird explains:

> Even though the early church did not have a strictly defined list of Christian writings that served as a theological authority for some time, they did have a definitive story that functioned as an authoritative guide. This story was the *regula fidei* or the "rule of faith." In a nutshell, the rule of faith is the narrative generated by the Jewish Scriptures and the Christian Scriptures. It is the story of creation, Jesus' birth, his life, his death and resurrection, the ascension, the beginnings of the church, and the consummation.[7]

The "rule of faith" summarized the story line of the apostolic teaching and protected the message of Jesus from corruption. In other words, the rule of faith secured what was essential to the Christian faith. It didn't say everything, but it did communicate the most important things. The early creeds, such as the Apostles' Creed and Nicene Creed, translated the narrative found in the rule of faith into central beliefs.[8] The Apostles' Creed, which affirms the core moments in the Christian story, originated in the late second or early third century and was put in its final form in the eighth century. The creed was, as Ben Myers labels it, "a grassroots confession of faith," "an indigenous form of the ancient church's response to the risen Christ."[9]

> I believe in God, the Father almighty,
> creator of heaven and earth.
> I believe in Jesus Christ, his only Son, our Lord.
> He was conceived by the Holy Spirit
> and born of the Virgin Mary.
> He suffered under Pontius Pilate,
> was crucified, died, and was buried.
> He descended to the dead.
> On the third day he rose again.
> He ascended into heaven,
> and is seated at the right hand of the Father.
> He will come again to judge the living and the dead.
> I believe in the Holy Spirit,
> the holy catholic Church,
> the communion of saints,
> the forgiveness of sins,
> the resurrection of the body,
> and the life everlasting.
> Amen.[10]

My (Josh's) church recites the Apostles' or Nicene Creed every Sunday, as does a chorus of millions around the world. In a sermon preached more than 1,500 years ago, Augustine told the people, "The Symbol [i.e., the creed] of the most holy mystery, which you received all together, and which you have given back today one by one, contains the words in which the faith of mother Church is solidly based on the firm foundation which is Christ the Lord."[11] The early creeds spell out what is essential to the gospel while leaving space on the main floor of Christianity for different rooms. The creeds act as a structural blueprint for the house, marking out the load-bearing walls. If you're in the midst of deconstruction but have followed us down to the main floor, don't start knocking down walls without examining them. Instead, use the creeds to help you find the important ones.

The Need to Embrace Patience and Mystery

The middle section of the creed focuses on Jesus and events in his life. Since we have already discussed Jesus and his resurrection in the previous two chapters, an example from the opening and another from the closing of the creed will suffice to suggest how main floor Christianity provides both stability and space to stand. Consider the opening sentence:

> I believe in God, the Father almighty,
> creator of heaven and earth.

The belief that God created all things is essential for Christianity. In contrast to the gods of ancient creation myths, the God of the Scriptures did not have a demiurge do his dirty work. Nor did the universe emerge through a cosmic battle between gods. God alone is the creator. Yet Christians diverge on questions of how and when God created it. You might have grown up in a church that taught that the earth is six thousand years old and that neither an "old" earth nor modern science can be reconciled with Christianity. Perhaps you were told that anyone who says otherwise was caving to the pressures of mainstream science, leaving their Christian faith in doubt. Such a stance, however, would mean that some of the world's most important Christian thinkers, several of whom we've met in this book, such as C. S. Lewis and Alvin Plantinga, would have to be dismissed.

This reactionary approach to scientific discovery is an example of a posture that Augustine warned against long ago: "There is knowledge to be had, after all, about the earth, about the sky, about the other elements of this world." After giving a long list of different things on earth and in the heavens, he adds, "and everything else of this kind. And it frequently happens that even non-Christians will have knowledge of this sort in a way that they can substantiate with scientific arguments or experiments."[12]

Augustine makes clear that non-Christians can know quite a lot about science. Then he describes the embarrassing situations in his own day in which certain Christians put too much into their own interpretations of the Bible in relation to science:

> Now it is quite disgraceful and disastrous, something to be on one's guard against at all costs, that they should ever hear Christians spouting what they claim our Christian literature has to say about these topics, and talking such nonsense that they can scarcely contain their laughter. . . . And what is so vexing is . . . that our authors should be assumed by outsiders to have held such views and, to the great detriment of those about whose salvation we are so concerned, should be written off and consigned to the waste paper basket as so many ignoramuses.
>
> Whenever, you see, they catch out some members of the Christian community making mistakes on a subject which they know inside out, and defending their hollow opinions on the authority of our books, on what grounds are they going to trust those books on the resurrection of the dead and the hope of eternal life and the kingdom of heaven, when they suppose they include any number of mistakes and fallacies on matters which they themselves have been able to master either by experiment or by the surest of calculations? It is impossible to say what trouble and grief such rash, self-assured know-alls cause the more cautious and experienced brothers and sisters.[13]

This quotation reminds us of recent works by historians, including David Hutchings and James Ungureanu, showing that many in the church are guilty of what Augustine has described. Hutchings and Ungureanu trace the supposed conflict between essential Christian teachings and modern science. Then they show how this "conflict" has been refuted by many scholars at multiple levels but lingers in popular consciousness, leading to polarization and angst.[14]

Consider the possibility that your Christian community has interpretive blind spots. If we accept two Christian ideas—that we are contingent and that we are sinful—it should lead to intellectual humility, and particularly so when we interact with the relationship between ancient texts and complex scientific theory. This is why, as Augustine explains, we need to be clear about the difference between essentials of the faith and our different interpretations of Scripture:

> And in discussing obscure matters that are far removed from our eyes and our experience, which are patient of various explanations that do not contradict the faith we are imbued with, let us never, if we read anything on them in the divine scriptures, throw ourselves head over heels into the headstrong assertion of any of them. Perhaps the truth, emerging from a more thorough discussion of the point, may definitively overturn that opinion, and then we will find ourselves overthrown, championing what is not the cause of the divine scriptures, when we should rather be wanting the cause of the scriptures to be our own.[15]

We could go on discussing the relationship between Christianity and science. We could even look deeper into Augustine's writings and see that despite not being privy to modern science, he has some fascinating ideas that are useful to us today.[16] However, our aim here is limited: we are recommending the same posture that Augustine long ago advised Christians to take. While standing firmly within the parameters of the rule of faith and the ancient creeds, humbly consider how others on the main floor have explored such questions and appreciate that many modern scientists have found a deep concord between their Christian faith and scientific discovery.

Next, we will skip to the closing section of the creed to consider a doctrine that has given many people reason to pause:

> He will come again to judge the living and the dead.

Judgment is another essential feature of the Christian story. The Scriptures and the creed teach that God is a righteous judge and his judgment will be a real event in history. Divine judgment has long been understood as more than metaphor. Even still, the Scriptures use metaphorical language to describe the reality of eternal judgment. Given the diverse biblical imagery portraying God's judgment, many have wrestled with how to best make sense of this doctrine. We can see this in ancient theological works like

Augustine's *City of God* as well as more recent contributions, such as Lewis's reflections on heaven and hell in *The Great Divorce* and N. T. Wright's proposal in *Surprised by Hope*.[17] Our aim here is not to analyze these proposals (we think some are stronger than others) but to help you see that searching for the right way to make sense of this doctrine does not disqualify you from living in the house of faith. However, knocking down divine judgment altogether does more than compromise the structural integrity of the house; as Christopher Watkin has observed, it also comes at a high cost to our shared humanity:

> The price to pay for losing the conviction of accountability to God is the sense that there exists an ethical meaning in the world that transcends myself. To seek to be free from divine judgment . . . is to find myself alone and unaccountable and to know that everyone else is in the same position.[18]

Destroying this wall would be bad news.

In the end, divine judgment finds its logic within the bigger story of a world where wickedness has gone wild. The righteousness of judgment fits with the human intuition that this world has gone absurdly wrong and something should be done. In a universe where a teenager walks into a school and begins shooting young children, in a society where young girls are still trafficked, in a world where Nazis murdered millions, something in us cries out for cosmic justice. We feel the same outrage in the ancient prophets, the psalmists, and the apostles, all of whom wrote longingly of a day of reckoning.

Will justice not be served in the end? Would a good God refuse to judge?

The instinctual response of many of us, however, is to reassure ourselves by pointing away from ourselves and those closest to us. Murderers, sex-traffickers, and Nazis are one thing, but me or Aunt Sally? The disquieting thought that we ask you to consider—and one that we all would rather quell—is that perhaps there is less separating us from these examples than we'd like to admit.

The Amazon series *The Man in the High Castle* takes place in America after World War II. Yet in this fictional telling, the Nazis have defeated the Allies and have invaded the United States. When we first meet the main character, John Smith, he is a brutal Nazi leader, torturing and killing innocent civilians. As the series goes on, we get more of the backstory, and a more complicated picture emerges. Smith is a family man who once served as an officer in America's armed forces. Once the Nazis dropped an atomic bomb on the United States, he had to choose: either risk his own death and the death of his family or join the enemy. He chose his family; he became a Nazi.

And then, with compromise after compromise, each one rationalized in its own way, he became a hollow shell of his former self, more monster than man, willing to torture and murder to stay in control. But as he played God, deciding for himself what was right and wrong, all in the name of safety and family, he spiraled deeper into a self-inflicted prison built from fear and pride. It's a horrifying story that in some sense demystifies wickedness. We can understand how Smith became what he became. We know all too well the temptations he succumbed to.

It could be that the series' creators even chose such a generic name for a reason: we are all John Smiths. He might as well have been called Adam. John Smith's story mirrors the ancient story told in Genesis 3, and the story has played over and over again. We all feel the desire to take control, the desire to be our own god, the desire to worship the created rather than the creator. It is terrifying and offensive to admit that the capacity for John Smith's appalling evil acts resides in each of us. Yet this runs along the lines of the witness of Genesis 3, which remains a deeply mysterious and inexhaustibly penetrating account of the psychology of evil and the distortion of human motivation.

The profound resonance of this story of human evil is surely one of the reasons the Christian story has lasted so long. Its principles have been played out time and again over the centuries, from King David's agonizing reflections over the fallout of his sin, to Paul's confession of the depths of his own depravity, to Augustine's psychological analysis of his own restlessness in *Confessions*. And each of us knows something of what they are talking about. For as offensive as the Christian doctrine of sin might sometimes feel, people across cultures and times have found in it something profoundly true about the human situation.

It is against this backdrop—a history of self-absorption, enmity, and violence—that divine judgment should be understood. This is why, as Lewis once pointed out, the ancients assumed not that God (or the gods) was on trial but that we are.[19]

And yet as the creed's own structure reminds us, a trial is not the end of the Christian story. The creed closes with everlasting life for those in Christ. The biblical story has always been marked by unmerited and unexpected grace. We see this grace even in the midst of the disastrous spectacle of Genesis 3: God unexpectedly provides for humanity and promises that the serpent will one day be defeated. By the closing chapters of the Bible, God fulfills his ancient promise to defeat evil.

This promise is ultimately fulfilled in what the writer J. R. R. Tolkien labeled the eucatastrophe, the moment in the history of the world in which God will enact his great reversal, when evil, in all its forms, will be defeated. Dostoevsky ironically puts this Christian hope on the lips of the skeptical Ivan in *The Brothers Karamazov*; he speaks of that day when every evil "will be healed and made up for," when "in the world's finale, at the moment of eternal harmony, something so precious will come to pass that it will suffice for all hearts, for the comforting of all resentments, for the atonement of all the crimes of humanity, of all the blood they've shed; that it will make it not only possible to forgive but to justify all that has happened with men."[20]

Let's return to one of the sources of doubt we alluded to in the preface: What about salvation for people outside of Israel before Christ came? Over the long history of Christianity, many different possible answers have been proposed. From our perspective, Augustine models a posture of humility worth emulating when reflecting on this concern. He cautions against rash, overconfident declarations while also insisting that however God works this out, the witness of Scripture is clear: Christ is the one and only mediator who can be trusted for salvation.[21]

Final judgment is our Creator's prerogative, not ours. Eternity is something we must trust God with, for we can't wrap our minds around how mercy and judgment will kiss in the end. But it will not be the first time people are surprised by how God has pulled the strands of justice and mercy together. No one was expecting the Messiah to die on a cross. No one was expecting the resurrection in the middle of human history. First-century Jews were not expecting that God would visit them as a human. As Tolkien pictures it, the Christian hope is that God will make everything sad come untrue.[22] How exactly this will happen we can't be sure. As a loving father asks his children to trust him, so our God asks us to look at Jesus hanging on the cross and trust that he will judge with perfect righteousness in the end. Who else could we trust to make all things right on the last day?

Although these two creedal affirmations—creation and judgment— are worthy of our attention by themselves, keep in mind the larger point of this chapter: the creeds help us locate and keep in place the load-bearing walls and reveal to us the ancient architecture of the main floor of the Christian house so that we can wonder as we confess with St. Paul that "we see through a glass, darkly" (1 Cor. 13:12 KJV).

Part Three

———

THE MAIN FLOOR

13

Wagering Wisely

IN CHAPTER 3 WE SAW how Montaigne responded to the contestability of the emerging modern world. He suggested that we should live lightly, pursuing a life of leisure and distraction. "Truth?" Montaigne says to us. "Who really knows?" Today he might say, "You be you." The secret to life is learning to be content with the world as it is rather than striving to touch the heavens.

Montaigne's skepticism led him to pursue an easygoing nonchalance. After all, why continue to feel angst about your beliefs if you cannot get to the truth anyway? The disillusionment caused by religious disagreements led Montaigne to reject hard commitments entirely. Many walking through deconstruction today can likely relate to these pressures. Montaigne's approach to life, as you might recall, got under René Descartes's skin. Descartes protested against this contingency, so he sought to lay and then build upon a foundation of certainty. Descartes thought he achieved this certainty by doubting everything and then reasoning his way up, one logical step at a time.

Some in the attic today have responded to modern contestability with a similar posture. Like Descartes, attic Christianity maintains extreme confidence in its own logic. Its certainty breeds rigidness, and this rigidness reinforces attic Christianity's overreach. Thus, individuals who grow up within the attic tend to believe that the attic itself is the totality of Christianity. The Bible is primarily used as a storehouse of data to support a rational system. Mystery and wonder are edged out. Christianity begins to look and feel different.

Around the same time that Descartes was working on his solution to the contestability of faith, a different approach was taken by our final guide to the main floor of the Christian house: the scientist-inventor-mathematician-philosopher-theologian Blaise Pascal. Pascal was an early paragon of the modern scientist, accomplishing more in his thirty-nine years than most polymaths would dream of doing in multiple lifetimes. In the midst of his work, Pascal saw with penetrating depth the problems being wrought by the modern world. With Pascal's help we will explore a posture that is neither in the spirit of Cartesian rationality nor haunted by the ghost of Montaignian skepticism.

Pascal's Problem with Descartes

Peter Kreeft notes that Pascal is "the *only* philosopher until the nineteenth century who did *not* climb onto Descartes's new methodological bandwagon . . . namely, trying to do philosophy and even life by the scientific method."[1] Pascal believed that questions about God and basic scientific questions should be answered in different ways. For Pascal, the heart—along with its desire for transcendent truth, beauty, and goodness—is essential to the human quest to discover meaning and purpose. Pascal called this "the logic of the heart." It's a logic deeply ingrained in humans and includes instinctive first principles like belief in the coherency and reliability of space, motion, numbers, and time, but also love.[2] These first principles of the heart cannot be proven in the way one proves a math problem, but they are nevertheless deep realities we assume and reason from.

Pascal was *not* saying that the logic of the heart is irrational. It does not contradict reason. In fact, Pascal was happy to give reasons one should believe that Christianity is true. However, he believed that the logic of the heart operated in dimensions that narrow Cartesian reason could never reach. Pascal offered a more expansive account of human rationality precisely because he understood the limits of the kind of reason that was gaining influence in his day.

Pascal said we should pay attention to the logic of the heart, with its desires and intuitions, when seeking truth, since moral intuitions and aesthetic sensibilities are woven into our perceptions of what is rational. If we attempt to bracket out the logic of the heart to gain certainty, we wager that a narrow kind of rationality is able to answer the big questions of life. But in fact, being reasonable means *doubting* reductionistic views of rationality. Or as the New York University professor Jonathan Haidt explains, "Human rationality depends critically on sophisticated emotionality. It is only because our emotional brains work so well that our reasoning can work at all."[3] Or consider what Iain McGilchrist, whose wide-ranging work combines neurological research and historical analysis, has to say: "Feeling is not just an add-on, a flavoured coating for thought: it is at the heart of our being, and reason emanates from the central core of the emotions, in an attempt to limit and direct *them*, rather than the other way about."[4]

Stop and consider which account of rationality is more reasonable to wager on. Can you prove that humans should love one another? The moral responsibility to love other humans and to treat them with dignity is self-evident to many people, but it isn't a truth that basic logic gives us. It is a deep moral conviction, but it can't be proven. Can we prove that humans should possess rights and be treated with universal dignity? That women should have the same rights as men? We cannot prove these things, but does that mean they aren't true?

In the hope of answering questions about God and eternity, should we attempt to escape our drive for the good and beautiful and whittle down our rationality to a brittle logic? Pascal would tell us not to bet on it. If an individual or society attempts to live with this type of rationality consistently, the result will be a growing cynicism toward the very things that make us human. As McGilchrist says rather bluntly, "The need for certainty is a sign of mental imbalance, and nothing is a greater waste of time than debating with someone who doubts everything, on the grounds that only certainty is admissible."[5]

Pascal's Problem with Montaigne

While Pascal used Montaigne to show the problems with rational dogmatism, he also found Montaigne to be dreadfully wrong about human nature. Pascal thought that Montaigne, by settling for skepticism and convincing himself that the fleeting happiness found in the pleasures of this world was enough, had developed a posture for life that would blind humans from reality and leave them in despair. Montaigne's medicine of diversions was like a prescription with horrible side effects; while promising to heal, it only made one's pathologies worse. In their recent work on modern restlessness, Benjamin Storey and Jenna Silber Storey sum up Pascal's point well:

> We engage in politics, in hunting and gambling, in flirting and text-messaging and much else, in an unceasing effort to get outside ourselves—we "cannot sit still in a room." For when we do, our minds inevitably turn to "the natural unhappiness of our weak and mortal condition, so miserable that nothing can console us when we think about it closely." What is so unhappy about our human condition? "We want truth and find only incertitude in ourselves. We seek happiness and find only misery and death. We are incapable of not wanting truth and happiness, yet we are incapable of either truth or happiness." Our consciousness of our mortality and our awareness of our own ignorance make us unhappy; we cannot learn to die, or rest our well-made heads on the pillow of ignorance, as Montaigne hopes. No psychic equilibrium is possible for a being whose desires so radically outstrip his possibilities. Misery follows ineluctably from an honest estimate of the gap between what we want and what we are.[6]

If Pascal could only see us now. The diversions available to us have multiplied in quantity and quality: eighty-inch 4K LED TVs, streaming services overflowing with content, and hyperrealistic video games to meet our demand for entertainment; exotic vacations to satisfy our thirst for adventure; and never-ceasing career paths ostensibly leading toward meaning and fulfillment. Our lives traffic in diversions that former generations couldn't have imagined. But Pascal wouldn't be surprised that collective discontentment is palpable in a world that clings to Montaigne's advice, a world that believes that if we only balance work and life *just* right, we'll be able to alchemize our entertainment, travel, and careers into self-actualization.

New York Times columnist David Brooks recently recounted his own journey through what he calls the first mountain of our contemporary Montaignian world. The first mountain "places the emphasis on self—individual success, self-fulfillment, individual freedom, self-actualization."[7] This focus on the self is the logical outworking of living with a deep skepticism about the world beyond what we can see. For if this world is all we can be sure of, and if we live only once, then why wouldn't we live for ourselves? Brooks points out the way in which

> the self has been the preoccupation of our culture—molding the self, investing in the self, expressing the self. Capitalism, the meritocracy, and modern social science have normalized selfishness: they have made it seem that the only human motives that are real are the self-interested ones—the desire for money, status, and power. They silently spread the message that giving, caring, and love are just the icing on the cake of society.[8]

But what happens when a whole society settles on the self, each person tending to their *own* gardens, with no second mountain to aim at or to bind them together with a vision that transcends the "me"? Brooks goes on to list what has happened (along with statistics and studies to support each): the loneliness crisis, social distrust, the crisis of meaning, tribalism, and sadness underneath a fragile veneer of happiness.[9] While Brooks addresses these pathologies directly, it's not surprising to see contemporary storytellers exploring them too.

The television series *The Morning Show* depicts the bitter disappointments waiting at the top of the first mountain.[10] Reece Witherspoon portrays a small-town girl from a broken home who becomes the host of a network morning show in New York City. It's the kind of rags-to-riches story Americans love. Admired by millions, she spends her days with the rich and famous, dreaming of using her platform to change the world. Then reality sets in. Her dysfunctional past leads to self-destructive behaviors. And beneath the glamour of her new job is a world of narcissism that treats fame, money, and power as its gods. Everyone is miserable.

While *The Morning Show* is set in our contemporary world, the story is old. Augustine shares in *Confessions* of his own disappointment with the first mountain. Recalling a trip to deliver a speech to the emperor, he writes, "My heart was issuing furnace-blasts anxiety over this assignment, and seething with fever of the obsessive thoughts disintegrating me from within, as I passed down a street in Milan and noticed a destitute beggar." The beggar was a drunk, finding illusory joy at the bottom of a bottle. Augustine realized that his desperate pursuit of achievement left him in worse shape—chasing his own illusory joy, living with "the many sufferings of [my] insanity."[11] The drunk man would sober up by the morning, but Augustine was to remain sozzled by his delusions, miserable and exhausted at heart.

Both *The Morning Show* and *Confessions* portray a world of false gods who make promises but always demand more. Pascal would tell us they are offering a mirage of diversions, restricting our ability to see the truth and truly flourish while binding us so that we serve their demands. In contrast with *The Morning Show*'s picturesque skyline luxury apartments overlooking the city or European villas opening up to vineyards, the reality inside is characters trapped in darkness, pain, and loneliness. Having turned in on themselves, settling for a salvation through the treasures they can see, they are a long, long way from true joy.

Diversions—either in the form of a carefully planned work-life balance or the all-out pursuit of a singular pleasure—can indeed temporarily distract us from the deeper aches we feel, but these diversions only hide from us a deep reality woven through creation. And being blind to this moral fabric of the universe, as well as to our true selves, will eventually only make us more restless.

Humans share a common longing for something more than what this world offers. About this longing Pascal would say that if you try to suppress your pining for something more—for a second mountain—you will lose something of your humanity. Now, neither we nor Pascal are arguing that this proves the existence of God. But if the Christian claim about God is true—if God is love and he has designed humans to flourish in his creation by rising above their self-absorption in order to radiate love outwards—then we shouldn't be surprised when our pursuit of worldly pleasures doesn't fully satisfy us. More on that in the next chapter. For now, consider the lesson Pascal is offering us: observing our own human nature gives us a realistic perspective on what it means for us to wager well in this life.

The Wager

Pascal famously proposed a "wager" to sober an audience drunk on diversions. Montaigne, scoffing at the possibility of reasonable faith, had persuaded many of Pascal's peers to avoid zealous commitment to any view and instead pursue worldly pleasures. The safest bet is no bet. But, Pascal asks, isn't that still a bet? Pascal's wager cuts through the complacency of those who imagine they are avoiding a wager altogether.

The truth is, we all must wager. Isn't it in your best interest to find the wisest *way* to wager?

Our Pascalian proposal is that the best way to wager is to take all of the aspects of human nature into account and ask this question: Where might true joy be found? Everything we know about humans and our world should be left on the table—especially the features of personhood that seem universal. We have a deep desire to believe what is actually true, not simply what we want to be true. We humans can't escape that our visions of love, beauty, meaning, hope, justice, and goodness are tied to how we reason. And each of these existential features of personhood is connected to the deeper experience of true joy; they are essential parts of a good life. In other words, by observing our human nature and a realistic view of rationality, we see that trying to answer and fulfill life's most fundamental questions about God requires that we give credence to our deepest longings, which is where true joy resides. Anything less would be a bad bet.

But then what about belief in God and Christianity? Including all these factors means that we can't escape into the narrow limits of scientific certitude to solve the question; we can't put God under a microscope or plug him into an equation. For many of us, this is an uncomfortable reality. In our pluralistic and disenchanted world, our imaginations are trained to think that anything that is reasonable can be discovered through a scientific process. But this assumption limits our horizons. As the Storeys observe, "The problem of belief is that, to eyes customarily fixed on tangible goods, material limits, and human honors, the promises of religion seem airy, thin, and implausible. To see them otherwise requires that we transform our vision transforming our desires—that is, by engaging with the animal, mechanical part of our natures."[12] This is why Pascal counsels those who are struggling to believe in God to "concentrate then not on convincing yourself by multiplying proofs of God's existence but by diminishing your passions."[13]

Pascal is not saying there is no place for evaluating the evidence for or against Christianity. Pascal himself argues that Christianity is "the most reasonable and most attractive explanation" for our lives.[14] But for Pascal, our reasoning is tied to our affections and imaginations, both of which have been twisted and blunted through bad motives and a misaligned social inheritance. In order to test Christianity, we will have to adjust our posture.

Recall Lewis's metaphor reminding us to look *at* and *along* the light of Christianity. We have talked to many people who left Christianity and who had indeed looked *at* it. Maybe this is you. Having considered many of the arguments for Christianity, you have walked away or are ready to do so. But it might be that the attic has caused you to take on a misaligned posture. Perhaps you've left an option untried—the main floor, where you can practice how to see and experience this deeper dimension of reality by looking *along* and stepping *into* its light.

Soon we will return to Pascal to retrieve and apply more of his observations. We will pair him with the work of contemporary psychologists and philosophers before suggesting some vision-restoring practices to try on. But Pascal also understood that most individuals struggling with doubt need more than *just* practices when striving to discover truth. People also need, as Lewis puts it, to continue looking *through* Christianity to see its explanatory power. In these ways, Pascal, like Lewis, nods to another option beyond rationalistic dogmatism or nonchalant skepticism. By asking us to follow a logic of the heart, Pascal suggests that we use our reason to consider what type of creatures we are and then do what is reasonable in light of these observations. The Christian claim is that looking through Jesus is the way to make sense of human nature and our most profound longings. By trying out Christianity on the main floor, we open ourselves up to see and embrace our humanity through an encounter with the ideal human. In the next chapter we will ask you to look again at some of humanity's deepest aspirations through the story of Christ.

14

A Window to See Through

AS WE LEARNED FROM PASCAL in the previous chapter, our humanity is laced with gut-level commitments that we aren't able to fully escape. He believed that rather than attempting to push aside these features of our personhood because we worry they will blind us from the truth, we should examine these intuitions as clues to life's meaning. Humans are like "a very strange shaped lock, with weird protuberances and indentations." In order to understand ourselves, we need "an equally strangely shaped key—that fits the lock."[1] Christianity offers such a key.

Or to return to our house metaphor, Christianity provides a window that makes sense of the world, including human nature and our deepest aspirations.

Justice

Across ideological and political spectrums, people are divided over what constitutes justice, but the desire for justice remains central. Two near-universal observations stand out:

- We live as if the notion of justice refers to something that is real.

- We recognize that the world is often unjust and sense that it should be otherwise.

These intuitions play out every day. People assume them to be true all the time on social media. One side will argue for gun control legislation because it is *not right* that individuals should be endangered by others' easy access to guns. On the other side, people argue against gun control legislation since it is *not right* to restrict one's freedom to defend herself. While each side has its own concept of justice, both sides share our two bulleted assumptions. Even when maintaining inherently unjust systems, humans feel an instinctive need to justify themselves. When slave owners, for instance, attempted to justify slavery, they appealed to property rights. Or when segregationists sought to maintain inequalities, their slogan was "separate but equal." Has any political movement ever self-identified as evil? Everyone wants to think of themselves as being on the right side of history.

This is why N. T. Wright refers to justice as a "broken signpost" that points us to God. The existence of justice seems at odds with a purposeless world, but as evidenced by the problem of evil, the brokenness of this signpost seems at odds with a purposeful world. What best explains our universal longing for justice alongside the human pattern of ignoring or distorting justice when doing so suits selfish ends?[2]

Some explain our desire for justice as an evolutionary development, suggesting that our moral intuitions evolved due to selection pressures favoring our human ancestors who worked well in groups.[3] If true, this would mean that our desires for justice were selected purely according to functionality and exist for our own benefit. It would also mean that justice is not based on any ultimate rationality or higher standard.[4] This leads to some disquieting implications. It would suggest that our appeals to justice are little more than social fabrications. How, then, could justice be anything other than a tool wielded by the loudest and most powerful members of society? If one assumes a natural order akin to survival of the fittest, wouldn't it be natural, even inevitable, for people to leverage justice to keep or put their tribe at the top of the pecking order? And after all, why shouldn't they?

But things appear different when you look at justice through the Christian window. A scientific description of moral formation is still maintained. Humans are selfish and often twist moral reasoning to achieve their own hidden ends. At the same time, Christianity affirms that our core desire for justice resonates with a mysterious reality behind the universe. Justice really matters, and it really exists. No amount of human twisting can pervert justice, because we do not define it. God does. Slavery, for example, is unjust not because we happen to believe so as a society but because each human being is made in the image of a God who loves them.

The Christian story also says that our central frustration with injustice has a solution. The recognition that we are unable to *ultimately* stop injustice is no reason to despair, because God promises final justice, not through human achievement but as a divine gift. The arc of the moral universe will one day arrive at a final justice, and that arc is not simply an illusion built by our posturing. Christians do not need to resign themselves to passivity or bitterness. They can look *along* Christianity and find reason to labor, lament, and hope.

We labor because God has called us to strive to reflect his justice in our daily lives. We lament because the belief that this world is unjust echoes back to the paradise we once had but have lost. We hope because we are honest enough to confess that final justice is not something we, being finite and fallen, can achieve but is rather something only a good God who sees and knows all will accomplish.

Dignity

Today in the West one of our highest ideals is that each person is unique and possesses inherent value and dignity. Historically, this is far from a universal aspiration. Aristotle thought some people were born to be slaves and some to be masters. It seemed self-evident to him that humans were *not* born as equals. Later, with the rise of modernism, some began to ask why humans should be viewed as fundamentally different from the "stuff" of the universe. Consider the words of the philosopher Thomas Hobbes:

> For seeing life is but a motion of limbs, . . . why may we not say that all automata (engines that move themselves by springs and wheels as doth a watch) have an artificial life? For what is the heart, but a spring; and the nerves, but so many strings; and the [joints], but so many wheels, giving motion to the whole body, as was intended by the Artificer?[5]

Hobbes's reduction of humanity to mere machines is "no innocent metaphor."[6] After all, if people are simply complicated machines, why should they be treated differently than other complicated machines? If we put cars to work for us, why not put some humans to work as well? We pull the levers of an excavator to achieve our ends. Are we comfortable pulling the levers of certain people to achieve those same ends? Is that right?

Few people today would go as far as Hobbes or Aristotle. But then, how is belief in universal and equal human dignity explained? If we attempt to root it in something functional— say, in our rational capacity or in our ability to form high-level relationships—we encounter serious problems. From simple observation we know that some people are smarter than others or have a larger capacity for deep relationships. And from a purely functional standpoint, some individuals are more valuable for serving the overall welfare of society.[7] It's difficult to escape the baggage that comes with a mechanical or functional view of human worth. What can make sense of this deep cultural aspiration that so many of us share?

Through the window of the Christian faith, the highest of human aspirations come into focus. Humans are not reducible to a set of mechanistic operations. Life is more than chemical reactions. We are more than the sum of various parts. We possess dignity as persons because we are made in the image of God. Human life is sacred and set apart in this universe. Humans are endowed with value because the creator of the universe loves them. No matter their station in life, each human is loved by God. This is how the grain of the universe was designed from the beginning: it is patterned after God, who, in his very essence, is love.

Beauty

Ivan, the skeptic in Dostoevsky's *The Brothers Karamazov*, at one point confesses, "I have a longing for life, and I go on living in spite of logic. Though I may not believe in the order of the universe, yet I love the sticky little leaves as they open in spring. I love the blue sky. I love some people, whom one loves you know sometimes without knowing why. I love some great deeds done by men, though I've long ceased perhaps to have faith in them. . . . It's not a matter of intellect or logic, it's loving with one's inside, with one's stomach."[8]

Despite his dogged rationalism, Ivan is a romantic at heart. But Ivan isn't alone. We all love and long for beautiful things: breathtaking ballads, the gallery of colors in autumn trees, the smile of a child, or, as Ivan says, "the great deeds done by men." Beauty has many iterations that hit us in the gut regardless of how we might theorize in our head.

As we continue to consider some of the core aspects of our humanity, here are a few observations about our relationship with beauty:

- We deeply desire to see, hear, and be around beautiful things.
- Beauty affects us in ways that reach beyond us in mysterious ways.

Beauty seems gratuitous, unnecessary for survival. It brings pleasure simply because it does, but it doesn't meet any *need*. If we were utterly deprived of beauty, we could go on surviving even as our souls shriveled. A person may survive while working nonstop in a bland and sterile office (just watch Apple TV's *Severance* to get a taste of what that would be like), but we all instinctively understand that any life stuck in a tasteless environment is impoverished.

Ivan recognizes that beauty makes life worth living, but his intellectual posture toward the world requires him to accept that the beauty he loves is of no real value. This is why he can say that even if he doesn't logically or intellectually believe in such beauty, he loves it. But given that our emotions and intellects work together to form our rationality, why not include this gut-level desire for beauty in our quest to answer the big questions of life?

Part of the answer is that we've inherited reductionistic forms of reasoning from our modern world and that this inheritance has collectively relegated beauty to the realm of cause-and-effect rationality we see in the natural sciences. Since beauty does not seem to have observable benefits for survival, it has become something eccentric to us. Ultimately, this kind of logic risks making beauty a "mere decoration for idle minds or a means of social control."[9] More specifically, one might explain the desire for beauty as a random result of evolutionary flukes. One could say, "Since symmetry often suggests health, your brain has been tricked into believing symmetry is more pleasing than asymmetry. It is just an odd trick of evolution. So, enjoy the experience of beauty. Why not? Just don't put much stock in it." But as N. T. Wright points out, how can you love beauty when you know it is "merely the accidental by-product of our evolutionary history, a vestigial memory of hunting prospects or mating opportunities?"[10]

But by looking *along* Christianity, the rays of beauty are seen as a reflection of God in our world. It is not a reflection in some flat sense; God does not look like a sunset or the *Mona Lisa*. No, beauty reflects God in that it pulls us out of ourselves. It shows us that there can be dimensions to life besides those that center on survival. It suggests a world that has been crafted by a creative God who values beautiful things. As Bart Ehrman says, it is difficult not to think of it as a gift.[11] But gifts are given by someone with intention. When looking through the Christian window, we see beauty pushing back against the malaise of a random, impersonal, and meaningless universe.

Finally, through Christ, beauty turns our eyes to the future, promising something beyond the pains of this world, beckoning us toward greater things to come.[12] J. R. R Tolkien infused his entire account of Middle-earth with this instinct. When Sam and Frodo cross Mordor, one of the darkest parts of the story, Sam looks up and sees a white star. "The beauty of it smote his heart, as he looked up out of the forsaken land, and hope returned to him. For like a shaft, clear and cold, the thought pierced him that in the end the Shadow was only a small and passing thing: there was light and high beauty forever beyond its reach."[13] When you look *through* Christianity, beauty has purpose. It points us beyond mere survival and toward a life of richer meaning.

Meaning

Wagering wisely in life means searching for an intellectually and existentially satisfying view of meaning and significance. As Augustine once explained, "Nobody in fact can live any style of life without those three sentiments of the soul; of believing, hoping, loving."[14] This is because the "logic of the heart" includes assumptions that humans have long recognized as being necessary for a meaningful life.

Our experiences with the glimmers of light we've briefly explored in this chapter seem to be shining beyond themselves and gesturing toward a profound and mysterious meaning. The Christian claim is that when Jesus broke into history, the flickering rays of light in which humans had long detected meaning—truth, beauty, goodness—were available to be seen anew, refracted through the window of Christ, shining with brighter and more vivid colors.

Jesus spoke directly to the human desire for truth. But he went further: he presented himself as the divine Logos, thereby subverting any depersonalized notion of ultimate truth. Truth was not an impersonal force or abstract system, but a person in the flesh.

The gospel story makes sense of the paradoxical nature of our beautiful and broken world. By becoming incarnate, God affirmed the goodness and beauty of this world; by dying and rising, Christ affirmed that our world is indeed broken but is worthy of redemption.

By embodying sacrifice, mercy, and justice, Jesus spoke to us as moral creatures. But then he went further, starting a moral revolution that has echoed through history. As we've seen, the modern West's assumptions about equal dignity and universal benevolence originated with Christ.

These rays of light do not prove God or Christianity. The secular frame of our world today certainly has its own explanations. Yet purely secular theories obfuscate the light that humans have long embraced, causing a certain "unease."[15] They have tended either to shrink back from the logical outworkings of their position or to move forward to reduce these sources of meaning to mere accidents and temporary illusions. The philosopher Bertrand Russell articulated these implications with unflinching clarity:

> That Man is the product of causes which had no prevision of the end they were achieving; that his origin, his growth, his hopes and fears, his loves and his beliefs, are but the outcome of accidental collocations of atoms; that no fire, no heroism, no intensity of thought and feeling, can preserve an individual life beyond the grave; that all the labours of the ages, all the devotion, all the inspiration, all the noonday brightness of human genius, are destined to extinction in the vast death of the solar system, and that the whole temple of Man's achievement must inevitably be buried beneath the debris of a universe in ruins—all these things, if not quite beyond dispute, are yet so nearly certain, that no philosophy which rejects them can hope to stand. Only within the scaffolding of these truths, only on the firm foundation of unyielding despair, can the soul's habitation henceforth be safely built.[16]

Perhaps Russell is right and this universe is vast, cold, and pointless. Maybe we find justice, human dignity, and beauty to be so inescapable because we have been duped. If so, we are left with few options except to despair, to make up meaning for ourselves, or, like Ivan, to commit to loving these things despite not believing them with our heads. But if you wager on the second or third choice, some questions remain: How meaningful is made-up meaning? What happens to such meaning when we are gone? What do we make of our individual meanings in the face of our own deaths and the inevitable death of the universe? Is separating logic from the heart sustainable in our actual lives? Charles Taylor describes the fragility of the situation: "Unsupported by a believable narrative, or by other earlier conceptions of order, the disciplined routines of everyday life in civilization become highly problematic. . . . They can come to seem a prison, confining us to meaningless repetition, crushing and deadening whatever might be a source of meaning."[17]

Even if you attempt to dismiss the rays of light and follow Russell's cold logic, you probably won't be able to shield yourself from them entirely. Light has a way of shining through. We intuitively live like our lives really matter; we all search for beauty; we all want to love and be loved. And ever since the light of Jesus's moral revolution penetrated into the deepest parts of our culture, it has seemed unnatural and difficult to revert back to a previous time and deny the aspirations that have led to the ideals of human rights and universal benevolence. We desire justice, and we sense that each person's life is sacred. Grounded in a historical claim and centered on a person, Christianity affirms, explains, and provides motivation to act on the deepest human ideals.

Where else can you find a story that does all that?

Part Three

———

THE MAIN FLOOR

15

"But I Still Can't Believe!
Now What?"

ONE TIME A GRADUATE STUDENT visited me (Josh) because she was struggling with debilitating doubts. I listened for some time as she anxiously described what was bothering her, and then we talked about those concerns. Toward the end our meeting, I gently asked her about her spiritual habits and church life. She replied that she had given up on church. It didn't help her intellectually, so she was now focused on finding the smartest people she knew to answer her questions. She didn't see the connection between her habits and her heart on the one hand and the doubts in her head on the other. And she didn't realize that she not only was being irrational about her own rationality but also had lost sight of what Christianity actually is and how it works.

So far, we've suggested that many of the pressures pushing you out of Christianity might lessen if you leave the attic and walk downstairs to the main floor of Christianity. We have also seen that the most popular destinations of those leaving the house have serious foundational and practical problems. And while never suggesting we have any definitive proofs, we have offered you reasons to believe in Christianity's foundational claims. At the very least, perhaps part 3 has reminded you that there are rational reasons for respecting the core claims of Christianity.

But maybe this is as far as you can go.

You might be thinking, "I am willing to grant you that by looking *at* and *along* Christianity, you've made a respectable case. You've reminded me why there are many intelligent people who believe and can offer intelligent reasons for their faith. But right now, these reasons aren't enough. Part of me would like to believe, but I still don't think I can muster any faith. So, now what?"

You aren't alone. Pascal addressed a similar situation over three hundred years ago:

> You want to find faith and you do not know the road. You want to be cured of unbelief and you ask for the remedy: learn from those who were once bound like you and who now wager all they have. These are people who know the road you wish to follow, who have been cured of the affliction of which you wish to be cured: follow the way by which they began. They behaved as if they did believe, taking holy water, having masses said, and so on.[1]

Taking some creative license, we will pick up on Pascal's suggestion and expand his practical advice in the next chapter. But first we need to acknowledge how crazy this might sound. Is Pascal really asking you to act as if you believe? Wouldn't that just be faking it? Hold on to those questions; we'll come back to them. First, join us in a quick thought experiment.

Imagine you are from another planet that does not have trees. On your visit to earth, when I introduce you to the idea that an acorn can transform into a tree, you find it preposterous. How might you come to believe in the tree-producing power of the tiny acorn? You could take my word for it when I say, "I've planted an acorn, watered it, and watched it grow into a tree." But let's imagine that there are acorn skeptics with other theories about the trees. They offer critiques that sound valid. After all, the acorn is small and looks nothing like a tree.

The solution to this thought experiment is straightforward: You could test out the "theory" for yourself. If you don't believe me, you could still plant the acorn, water it, and see what happens. Even if you find yourself with a sliver of belief that my claim is true, the way ahead is the same: plant, water, and watch.

If you'd like to believe in Christianity but you don't think you can, you might be going about things the wrong way. It could be that you have been trying to control contingencies in order to achieve a kind of certainty, your own two-plus-two approach to the God question. But the wrong method with wrong expectations almost inevitably leads to frustration.

The claim of Christianity is not simply that its story offers a way to explain our lives and the world, though as we've seen, we believe it to have unrivaled explanatory power that we can look *through*. Nor is Christianity only claiming that God has entered the world in the person of Jesus and has risen from the grave, though this is a foundational historical claim that we have looked *at*. Christianity also claims to offer ways for you to commune with God and flourish in a broken world and beyond.

Through the contingencies of history and the experiences of life, God breaks through so that you can grow in faith. In this chapter we will see how discerning the truth requires us not just to look *at* and *along* but also to step *into* the light and practice the ways of faith. To see why this is so, we will need to pull on some threads from the previous chapters.

The Problem of Unbelief

What we are able to believe is not determined in a social vacuum.

A holistic picture of what goes into the psychology of belief is related to what Charles Taylor has called the "social imaginary." It refers to "our sense of things," and not simply what we believe but rather "the way the universe is spontaneously imagined, and therefore experienced." It is usually "not expressed in theoretical terms, but is carried in images, stories, and legends."[2] Working powerfully in the background of our lives, our social imaginary frames what we spend our life thinking about, what we can imagine as possible, and how we see the world around us.

Recall from chapter 3 the term "disenchantment," a word we used to describe how in many corners of the modern world people are conditioned to imagine that the material world is in no way charged with sacred meaning and spiritual activity. Andrew Root explains the challenge this causes for sustaining belief:

> In the modern era our attention has been drawn away from what our ancestors thought was obvious: that a personal God acts and moves in the world. Some would say this movement represents liberation: we've put aside an untenable belief. . . . [Instead, what] we've acquired [is] a unique observation blindness. It's not that we've given up an untenable belief but that [our secular age had] drawn our attention away from divine action and toward something else. New forms of attention make us unable to see what was once obvious.[3]

Root puts his finger on what could be the heart of your problem. As the psychologist Richard Beck explains, "Faith is a matter of perception. Faith isn't forcing yourself to believe in unbelievable things; faith is *overcoming attentional blindness*."[4] Or as Beck says later, "Disenchantment is often a sign that you've lost touch with the aesthetic, ineffable aspects of the faith. If you're struggling with disenchantment, odds are you are *thinking* rather than paying *attention*."[5] If Beck is right, it might mean you have to recalibrate how you are dealing with your doubt. It also means that Pascal, writing when disenchantment was just beginning to emerge, was on to something long before the philosophers and professional psychologists of our day.

Self-Delusion or True Rationality?

We're now better able to consider the sanity of Pascal's advice and the questions we raised earlier. Isn't stepping inside of the light to try on certain practices *while still having serious doubts* just self-delusion? Wouldn't we be playing pretend for no good reason?

To answer both questions as straightforwardly as possible: no. Here's why.

First, there are good reasons to take the core claims of Christianity seriously. We aren't asking you to try on something that doesn't have intellectual merit. As we've seen, there are logical, historical, and existential reasons both to respect and to wager on Christianity.[6] These reasons do not operate in a historical vacuum, and a variety of factors will cause different people to find them more or less persuasive. Nonetheless, they work together to justify at least wagering on the possibility that Christianity is true.

To return to the analogy of the acorn, you had a reason—namely, my testimony—to make a wager by taking concrete actions (planting, watering, and watching). This is similar to what Iain McGilchrist has observed about faith in general: "There is nothing blind about faith, but there is nothing certain about it, either. It is like trusting the outstretched hand that helps you ford the stream: you see the stream, you see the hand; you do not blindly step, but step you must."[7] Even if you don't have much faith, or perhaps none at all, you have good reasons to step out and try Christianity on again. And this time you will be trying it on outside the attic and, as we will see in the next chapter, with some new (but actually old) practices at your disposal.

Second, what other options do you have? We saw in our interaction with Rhett McLaughlin in chapter 8 that we are all formed by the cultural artifacts we consume as well as the communal practices and narratives we inhabit. We can't escape this reality. But we can imagine—wrongly—that we somehow live outside these contingent realities, that we aren't breathing in the habits, stories, and symbols that constitute our cultural air. But doing so would mean simply turning a blind eye to the truth.

James K. A. Smith uses the word "liturgies" to refer to the communal practices and patterns of behavior that all societies, even secular ones, inevitably develop, such patterns forming the hearts and minds of the citizens.[8]

Let's do another thought experiment. Imagine that you are a time-traveling alien who's also an anthropologist of religion.[9] You land in Europe during the Middle Ages, and you discover, in the words of Paul from Acts 17, that these people are "in every way . . . very religious" (v. 22). The people flock to churches. The cathedrals are bustling centers of life in every major city. The saints of old are depicted in stained-glass windows lining the walls, inspiring the veneration of the people worshiping there. The faithful gather to hear the priests tell sacred stories that give their life meaning and hope. Holy books are revered, and those who have the means and ability crouch around them for study and prayer. Those who can afford it go on pilgrimages to holy places and are met by festive throngs upon arrival.

Then you hit your time-traveling button and arrive in the most secular parts of today's earth. To your surprise you discover these people, too, are "in every way . . . very religious." You find people gathering in cathedrals known as malls, walking down expansive aisles and looking, not at saints in stained-glass windows, but at mannequins in shopfronts modeling the good life. Pilgrims flood to the largest cities and congregate to celebrate yearly festivities called the Super Bowl, the World Series, and the NBA Championship. Worshipers clutch their illuminated holy devices that are designed to direct them not to the heavens but to themselves. In the evenings they don't gather to hear sermons but worship alone before screens, enraptured by stories of the good, true, and beautiful. They don't sing hymns pointing to God, but they cover over silence with song after song promising them that the next romantic relationship will at last fulfill them.

Smith's work makes a compelling case that even if someone doesn't believe in God, opting out of "liturgies" isn't really an option. We are liturgical by nature.[10]

By trying out the practices we suggest in the next chapter, you won't be moving from zero formative practices in your life to a large collection of them that suddenly color your vision. Your vision is already colored by many liturgies. If you take Pascal's wager, you will at least be consciously adopting practices that have an ancient pedigree. If you step into these practices, you will be accepting the possibility that followers of Jesus have collectively discovered and passed down ways of attending to God's presence. Listening to the Christians living on the main floor is like listening not just to one person but to multitudes of people through time and space telling you that they have stepped into the light of Christianity and experienced a mysterious and transformative grace.

Third, since we can't opt out of formative practices altogether, the question becomes which practices best form us for flourishing. This means that rather than only comparing the logic of Christianity with the alternatives, we can also compare Christianity with other ways of life, asking, What is the path to true joy? Or, What practices lead to human flourishing? After all, if Christianity is true, and if Jesus was sincere when he promised that it was better for him to go away so that the Spirit might come (John 16:7), then shouldn't Christianity in some sense "work"?

Consider how Pascal's advice makes sense given the nature of our situation. Like the scientist that he was, Pascal set out to observe humans as we are, not in the abstract but in real life. What are the discernible facts on the ground? We have already seen how Pascal critiques Montaigne's practice of distracting himself from his own unhappiness. This unhappiness is rooted in what Pascal observes as the great paradox of our existence: humans are both wonderful and wretched animals.

We humans have used our abilities to make both vaccines and atomic bombs. We perform altruistic acts of charity and sadistic deeds of hatred. In our own hearts we desire to love but are plagued by petty jealousies. More specifically to Pascal's point, our misery itself is evidence of our greatness. For a cat does not suffer philosophical or existential misery. Cats don't feel frustrated with themselves for not rising up to achieve a greater moral status. They don't reflect on their inevitable deaths, nor do they search desperately for a way to escape the absurdity of life. Cats appear quite content in their "catness."

In other words, our ability to live highly moral lives, and even more so our deep intuition that we should, is what makes us great. But it also makes us troubled. We experience "the miseries of a great lord, the miseries of a deposed king."[11] Riffing off Pascal, the Storeys explain that we humans, unlike other animals,

> want happiness, love, and approbation, yet wherever we turn in human life, we find ourselves facing another example of our sad and hateful emptiness. We want truth, yet we cannot even grasp the truth of ourselves, for an enormous contradiction lies at the heart of our being. And yet, try though we might, we cannot stop ourselves from desiring the happiness and truth that perpetually fly from our grasp.[12]

Pascal thinks that if we refuse to acknowledge this paradox, we can't really know ourselves. Admitting that this uncomfortable diagnosis lines up with the human experience is a necessary step in finding a true cure.

In some sense modern capitalism is built around finding a cure. This is understandable. For if we find ourselves naturally unhappy but desiring to be happy, it's only logical to seek a cure. This is why successful brands promise a cure and mimic religion in the process. As Naomi Klein explains, drawing on her research on successful brands, humans seek "community and narrative and transcendence"; the most effective campaigns seek to convince us that we can get these things if we just "go shopping again."[13]

As we saw earlier, Montaigne offered diversions as a cure. Diversions can at least distract us as we learn to accept the futility of striving for a higher existence. But Pascal observed that these diversions weren't working, and he predicted they never ultimately would. Our nature is not simply to settle in and be content with trivialities and moral indifference. Trying to live like that will only lead to more restlessness. This is why, even in a world that has implicitly embraced Montaigne's logic, there are signs of religious fervor bubbling up in even the most secular environments. From the rise of identity politics, to the zealous evangelism of social activism, to SoulCycle fervor, religious-like devotion is alive and well.

With all this in mind we should be asking what best explains these unsettling but honest observations about our nature as humans and what kind of deep commitments and practices will actually bring healing. Christianity gives an answer to both of these questions. First, humans are made in the image of God but have rebelled against the one whose image we bear. This fits with the paradoxes we observe in our own existence. Second, Christianity offers the cure for the human situation.

At this point Pascal asks, What do you have to lose by wagering on Christianity, patiently trying on new (but actually old) practices? What will you be giving up by trying? A few more years or decades of living in the diversions of consumerism and consumption? Or a life of cobbling together your own meaning under the shadow of doubt and certain death? In contrast, think about what you stand to gain by seriously seeking God and stepping into the practices of main-floor Christianity.

Surprised by Joy

The testimony of countless Christians is that certain practices have served as means by which to experience God. Either over a "long obedience in the same direction"[14] or in surprising palpable experiences of his presence, throughout history billions have testified to having planted, watered, and watched—and then having encountered the grace of God. This is true of both of us as well as the three guides we've heard from while touring Christianity's main floor. Our guides took the intellectual side of the faith seriously, and in different ways, each witness to having experienced God's presence: from Augustine's *Confessions*, to Pascal's two-hour experience with God ("Fire . . . *joy, joy, joy, tears of joy*"[15]), to the fulfillment Lewis found in God after a long search for joy. We don't mean to imply that attending to God always leads to an experience as vivid or intense as the ones described in the more dramatic testimonies. But the collective witness of his people and the Scriptures is that those who humbly continue to seek God will eventually find him.

16

Practicing Your Way
through Doubt

CHRISTIANITY IS NOT JUST ABOUT doctrines and beliefs. It is a way to inhabit the world.

As Alan Jacobs has observed from C. S. Lewis's life, though doctrines are "absolutely necessary as maps toward one's true destination—they should never be the *goal* of the Christian life."[1] Many of us get this wrong. The modern world has done much more than challenge our doctrines; it has changed the way we see the faith and has shifted the way we attend to the world. "Christian living" is reduced to ideas. God is relegated to "up there" in the "supernatural," while our daily lives take place here in the "natural" world.

Yet if Christianity is true, these vision problems, so to speak, will screen out certain realities.[2] We need to think about this problem—but that can't be all we do. Our thinking should prompt us to pay better attention.

In his final book, Lewis observed, "We may ignore, but we can nowhere evade, the presence of God. The world is crowded with Him. He walks everywhere *incognito*. And the *incognito* is not always hard to penetrate. The real labour is to remember, to attend."[3] Main-floor Christianity has long claimed that "the God who created all things out of love has given us a world full of meaning"[4]—that is, a world full of signs.

What if God is present but we have inherited a way of seeing that blinds us to his activity? What if we are under a spell, conditioned by the hustle and bustle of our modern lives, and thus don't see him at work all around us?

You might think you've already tried Christian practices. After all, if you grew up in the church, this is all old hat, right? Well, maybe not. It could be you have adopted some slanted practices. We aren't suggesting you adopt the practices discussed below as a list of do's and don'ts. This isn't about checking your quiet time off a list, or getting more data about God into your head, or vowing to listen only to Christian music. Rather, these practices have the potential to pierce through the noise of our modern world. They just might redirect your attention to the joy we humans deeply desire.

If you want to try and live on the main floor of Christianity but only try on main-floor *ideas*, you're not doing it right. Doing it right means trying out main-floor *ways*, and the collective wisdom of the main floor offers many ways to practice your way through doubt to a deeper faith.

1. Participate in the Sacred

The disenchantment of our modern world is not absolute. There are moments of enchantment that even the most ardent naturalist would struggle to dismiss, times when the sacred leaves us longing for more. This is part of the confusing cross-pressured air of our day.[5] Even the most secular of cultures feel a deep need to recognize birth, death, and marriage as charged with a deep significance.

Next time you get a chance, hold a newborn baby and take a moment to reflect. Marvel at the preciousness of new life. Ponder its wonder and frailty. Allow yourself to experience the existential weight of the moment. Where did this human life come from? What is the meaning of her existence? Do we have a duty to protect her? If so, who gave us that duty? What would it mean to ignore that duty? Does something inside of you rebel at the very thought? The birth of a new human is a moment of profound meaning, and it seems natural and necessary to sacramentalize that moment.

Just as the beginning of a life gestures toward a sacred reality, the end of life calls us to memorialize life as meaningful. For our loved ones "are so significant to us, they seem to demand eternity."[6] This is why, as Charles Taylor observes, "even people who otherwise don't practice have recourse to religious funerals; perhaps because here at least is a language which fits the need for eternity, even if you're not sure you believe all that."[7] Perhaps this is also why the teacher of Ecclesiastes tells us to prefer funerals over parties (Eccles. 7:2). Death breaks the illusion of this life's permanency, and it confronts us with questions that we by ourselves do not have answers for. It humbles us. If we allow it to, reflecting on the reality of death can focus our attention.

On a brighter note, attend a wedding. When the bride and groom are exchanging vows, it is easy to imagine that we live in a universe meant for love. While Richard Dawkins might tell you that our world is one of blind indifference, the beauty and "rightness" of weddings motion to a different story. Perhaps this is partly why we have experienced such a cultural firestorm over marriage. For those demanding the legality of same-sex marriages, legal civil unions aren't enough. These controversies signal that people today still sense the sacredness of the ideal of marriages as a lifelong commitment of love. Christians have ancient ways of expressing these bonds, linking marriage to a divine logic of love and stamping this commitment with eternal meaning.

With respect to birth, death, and marriage, the collective wisdom of the church has passed down to us communal practices that signify the holiness of the events and attend to their deeper significance. Step into them with your eyes wide open.

2. Commit to a Room in the House That Is Serious about Worship

The church, a community of believers covenanted together, is the means by which faith grows and is nurtured. The church exists for worship in response to God. These are, at least, the historic claims of Christianity.

Even on days when we are having trouble believing, by submitting ourselves to exhortation from the Holy Scriptures and the proclamation of Christ, we are wagering on the promise that the Word will not return void. For thousands of years the Spirit has been calling people into the story that satisfies the paradoxes of life—weaving together goodness and justice, beauty and wretchedness, responsibility and grace—while redirecting our lives toward our deepest and truest love.

Main-floor Christianity has long maintained that when we participate in Communion, taking part in the Lord's body and blood, God is at work in a special way. Debates about how exactly he works through the sacrament continue between different rooms in the Christian house. Yet the consensus on the main floor is that God not only visually reminds us of the gospel through the Lord's Supper but also mysteriously restores the eyes of our hearts.

Corporately learning the cadence of the Psalms, the church's prayer book, is also an important spiritual practice. Their serious worship expresses the range of human emotions and situates them within the big picture of redemption. In doing so, the Psalms both affirm the significance of our emotions and direct them forward to their proper ends. This does not mean that worship involves only chanting the Psalter. Rather, the Psalms offer an example that refuses to flatten worship into simply celebration, for this would mean dealing with doubt and disillusionment by means of a facade. Find a church that praises God for the good gifts of creation, laments the evils of this world, confesses their sins, sings of God's steadfast faithfulness, and points forward with resolve to the hope of new creation. Even when you cannot muster a smile or the will to sing yourself, still go. Listen to the words. Watch as the bread is broken and the wine is poured. Pay close attention to the Scriptures.

3. Slow Down and Pray

The Ignatian Examen is an ancient prayer originally drawn from the writings of St. Ignatius of Loyola. This prayer is designed to slow you down and help you notice parts of your day where God was working. This practice will train your heart and mind to attend more carefully to the presence of God in your daily life. The prayer has five main parts:[8]

- In a quiet and secluded moment, think back through your day and take note of all that you have to be grateful for. Thank God for each of these things with a serious awareness that these gifts are not assured for any of us. This moment of thanksgiving pushes back on the spiritual exhaustion that can so often accompany our stressed and hectic lives.
- Ask God to work through this time of prayer to open your eyes so you can see how he is at work in and through your life.
- Prayerfully look back on your day. Examine the stirrings of your heart. Pay attention to what in your day made you turn toward God and what in your day made you turn inward, toward your own interests and desires. What parts of your day made the lives of others better or worse? Attend carefully to how you feel about the way your day progressed.
- Ask God for forgiveness for any actions of selfishness, envy, laziness, or rage. Reflect on the God who has forgiven you and loves you through Christ.
- Look forward to tomorrow and ask God to guide you in living in accordance with his will.

4. Meditate on (Not Just Study) Scripture

Lectio divina is the ancient practice of contemplative Scripture reading. If you grew up in a community in which people saw Scripture reading through the lens of data mining, this might feel odd to you at first. *Lectio divina* is not simply about learning. It is about interacting with God.[9]

Like the Ignatian Examen, *lectio divina* begins in a quiet and secluded moment. Read (*lectio*) Scripture slowly, paying attention to the entirety of the passage. Then reflect (*meditatio*) on what the passage means for your daily life. This will be different for every passage of Scripture, but it will always involve reflecting on both the meaning of the text and the current state of your own life. How does the text speak to your life?

Next, respond (*oratio*) to God. Talk to him. Disagree or complain; thank him or question him. Tell him how you will implement his teaching in your own life. Finally, rest (*contemplatio*). This one may be the most foreign to you. After responding to God, just be with him. Sit in his presence. Passively observe, and simply rest. "Be still, and know that I am God" (Ps. 46:10).

5. Spend More Time Touching Grass

Our daily lives have too often been eroded by the acids of efficiency and productivity dripping from the machinery of meritocracy. In a society where we constantly feel the drive to hurry up and to instrumentalize the world around us, slowing down and taking a walk can open us up so we can see more.

Christianity has always held that the natural world cries out to us about God. So, take a walk, enjoy the fresh air, marvel at a waterfall, wonder as you gaze upon a starry night. These, too, are signs, working on us at a visceral level and pointing beyond ourselves. This is why, in Lewis's fictional *The Screwtape Letters*, a demon who is experienced in destroying the faith of humans chastises his younger counterpart: "You allowed him to walk down to the old mill and have a tea there—a way through country he really likes, and taken alone. . . . How can you have failed to see that a *real* pleasure was the last thing you ought to have let him meet?"[10] In contrast to the cheap gratification found in the trivialities of consumerism and the use of technology to build little worlds around ourselves, such real pleasures ground us to reality and diminish our appetite for hollow pursuits.

Augustine encourages us, "If sensuous beauty delights you, praise God for the beauty of corporeal things, and channel the love you feel for them onto their Maker."[11] If you limit yourself by coldly viewing nature as a brute reality to be manipulated or as ends to be loved for themselves, they will eventually prove to be a source of sorrow. For the flower fades, and nature will not love you back. But if you learn to delight in beauty as a gift, the greater reality of the giver and the warmth of his embrace will become easier to see and feel.

6. Continue to Look *At* and *Along* the Faith

This last practice is something we have been doing throughout this book. By looking *at* Christianity, we've seen reasons for belief. By looking *along* Christianity at our world, we've seen how the Christian story makes sense of our lives and the world around us. Go back through books like this one. Follow our endnotes to other resources. And by all means continue to think deeply about the faith. But don't forget: our intellectual vision is connected to the habits we develop, the communities we inhabit, and things we choose to pay the closest attention to.

Wagering on Grace

Without claiming a mechanistic and universal demonstration of the truth of Christianity through these practices, in this chapter we've been inviting you to wager on Christianity by developing habits that allow you to step into its light. If there is a God and Christianity is true, these practices are some of the means of experiencing his grace. Our challenge to you is to try them out and persevere in them. Why wouldn't you?

If you say, "Because I fear being duped," at least admit that you are allowing fear to control your decision. But more importantly, realize you are making a decision that will not protect you from what you are afraid of. As we've seen, attending to the world, even in the most secular ways possible, can never be neutral, and it includes liturgies that are already shaping your rationality and judgments. None of us can escape the risk of being duped.

Yet fear makes us do ill-advised things, including making bad bets, such as insisting that you can escape your own contingency despite the overwhelming evidence that this can't be done. The theologian Sarah Coakley has detected beneath this ill-advised wager a fear of losing control and of the pain that such loss may bring. During an interview with an agnostic television host who inquires about how he might discover God, she explains why practicing the faith is so vital to cutting through the lie that has long placed scales over the eyes of the human race: our dogged confidence in our own autonomy:

> I as a believer find that it is in silent waiting on God that ultimate transcendent reality impinges on me. And every time I do that, I think of it as a kind of rehearsal for the moment when I finally have to give over control, which will be the moment when I die. . . . I think rehearsing for death is actually one of the most important things we do as humans, because once we're no longer afraid of death, then we're no longer afraid of life.
>
> And you strike me as a person who is very interested in controlling what you believe in for fear that . . . you would no longer be in charge, the captain of your own soul. But when you come to think of it, there's going to come a day when you're lying in bed, about to die, and that possibility will no longer be a fantasy that you can maintain.[12]

In some ways each of the practices in this chapter are meant to unmask the fantasy of being in the captain's seat and somehow protecting yourself from pain, for in holding on to this fantasy you might just be shielding yourself from true happiness. Wagering on Christianity means learning to let go of such illusions by adopting certain practices. By confessing through word and deed your own contingency each day—including your lack of control over the gifts you receive, the pain you've suffered, and the eventual death you cannot escape—you begin to see past the delusions of your own pride. Such a posture is what the Christian Scriptures repeatedly say is required for receiving his grace. "God opposes the proud, but gives grace to the humble" (James 4:6 NRSV).

This has been a hard lesson for both of us, but it is a lesson that might give you hope: The pains of doubt might just be God's invitation to a posture that opens your life up to experience his presence. For the God who entered the world as a baby, died on a cross to conquer death, rose from the grave, and mysteriously permits evil for an undecipherable good is surely able to use even your doubts for such a sacred purpose. If so, the surprise of doubt may turn out to be the means by which you receive a very different kind of surprise: joy.

EPILOGUE

Praying with the Dead

I (JOSH) HAVE LANGUISHED through seasons in which praying has felt almost impossible. Growing up in an evangelical church in the American South, I assumed prayer needed to be extemporaneous. I inherited the idea that if I was going to experience the presence of the Lord, *I* needed to generate words spontaneously. When I couldn't find the words, when my mind wandered, when my attention flickered, I gave up. These desolate seasons of prayerlessness led to agonizing doubts—both intellectual and existential.

A turning point came when I let others help me pray. I began to mouth the prayers passed down to me from the dead. I began praying the Psalter. I also began praying ancient prayers, such as those found in Augustine's *Confessions* as well as *The Book of Common Prayer*. I became an apprentice to the departed. Through their words I began to speak to God and learned to listen.

But it hasn't been only the dead whom I have prayed with. I've needed the prayers of the living as well. Douglas Kaine McKelvey's two volumes of prayers, entitled *Every Moment Holy*, have put words to the experiences of my life, and I commend these prayers to you.[1]

Through them I have felt the Lord's presence. Yet even still, as Mc-Kelvey has written,

> There are other moments, as now,
> when I cannot sense you near, cannot hear you, see you,
>   touch you—times
> when fear or depression or frustration
> overwhelm,
> and I find no help or consolation, when the seawalls of my
>   faith crumble
> and give way to inrushing tides of doubt.[2]

As I have repeated these words, I've realized that I am not alone. I have prayed with McKelvey as he calls upon a cloud of doubting witnesses:

> Even as the patriarch Job
> made of his pain and confusion a petition;
> even as the psalmists again and again
> carried their cries, their questions, their laments
> to you; so would I be driven by my doubts
> to despair of my own strength and knowledge
> and righteousness and control,
> and instead to seek your face, knowing that
> when I plead for proof,
> what I most need is your presence.[3]

What we most need is God himself. Through such prayers, you too might learn to sense his presence. Yet as I wrote in the preface, I still have moments when I feel the pressures of doubt. Through the years I have come to see how these struggles have a place in God's providence:

> O Lord, how many times have you graciously
> led me through doubt into a deeper faith?
> Do so again, my Lord and my God!
> Even now. Do so again!

You alone are strong enough
to carry the weight of my troubled thoughts,
    even as you alone are strong enough to bear
    the burden of my sin and my guilt and my
    shame, my wounds and my brokenness.

O Christ, let my doubts never compel me to
hide my heart from you. Let them rather arise as
questions to begin holy conversations.
Invert these doubts, turning them to invitations
to be present, to be honest, to see you, to cry
out to you, to bring my heart fully into the
struggle rather than seek to numb it.

Let my doubts become invitations to wrestle
with you through such dark nights of the soul—
as Jacob wrestled with the Angel—until the day
breaks anew and I am fresh wounded by your
love and resting in the blessing of peace again in
your presence.[4]

I pray you will join us in wrestling with and waiting on the Lord. For as it turns out, wounds can have their purposes.

The desolate winter turns into a flourishing spring. The darkness of night is interrupted by the glimmering rays of the rising sun. Tears of grief over loss are followed by cries of joy over new life. The suffering of the cross presses forward to the resurrection of the dead. This is the story of the world. This is Christ's story. For Jesus's followers, this is our story as well.

We all must live somewhere. Each day we put our life on the line through practices, wagering on some way. Will you join us in wagering on the One who claimed to be "the way and the truth and the life" (John 14:6)? Where else will you go to find "the words of eternal life" (John 6:68)?

ACKNOWLEDGMENTS

A special thanks to those who read drafts of this book and helped improve it: Connor Schonta, Karen Swallow Prior, Jonathan Pennington, Mark Allen, John Yates III, members of the Center for Pastor Theologians in the St. Anselm Fellowship, and, of course, our keen editors at Brazos, Katelyn Beaty and Eric Salo.

NOTES

Preface

1. Christopher Watkin, *Biblical Critical Theory: How the Bible's Unfolding Story Makes Sense of Life and Culture* (Grand Rapids: Zondervan, 2022), 113.
2. C. S. Lewis, "Christian Apologetics," 1945, available at https://virtueonline.org/christian-apologetics-cs-lewis-1945.
3. Lewis, "Christian Apologetics."
4. John Cottingham, *How to Believe* (New York: Bloomsbury, 2015), 8.

Chapter 1: This Isn't How They Told Us It Would Be

1. To protect the identity of my friends, I have provided pseudonyms and adjusted some of the superfluous details of the stories recorded here.

Chapter 2: An Invitation to Explore the House of Faith

1. C. S. Lewis, *Mere Christianity* (1943; repr., New York: Macmillan, 1960).
2. Abigail Favale, *The Genesis of Gender: A Christian Theory* (San Francisco: Ignatius, 2022), 19.
3. Favale, *Genesis of Gender*, 19.
4. Mark A. Noll, *The Scandal of the Evangelical Mind*, with new preface and afterword (Grand Rapids: Eerdmans, 2022), 170.
5. For more on evangelicalism, including its global expressions, see John G. Stackhouse Jr., *Evangelicalism: A Very Short Introduction* (New York: Oxford University Press, 2022).
6. Brian Zahnd, *When Everything's on Fire: Faith Forged from the Ashes* (Downers Grove, IL: InterVarsity, 2021), 28.
7. Alvin Plantinga, *Warranted Christian Belief* (New York: Oxford University Press, 2000), 63.

Chapter 3: Looking Back to Look at the Attic

1. Tom Holland, *Dominion: How the Christian Revolution Remade the World* (New York: Basic Books, 2019), 541.
2. Charles Taylor, *A Secular Age* (Cambridge, MA: Harvard University Press, 2007), 26.
3. See Alec Ryrie, *Unbelievers: An Emotional History of Doubt* (London: William Collins, 2019), 44–74.

4. In this period we've singled out elements that blended together to form the atmosphere of contestability and disenchantment so prevalent in our world today. History is, of course, much messier than these quick summaries can capture. If we had more time, we would show how the printing press and other technological, economic, and political changes also played major roles. But remember, this is only an all-too-brief sketch. We have singled out a few significant factors for our purposes here. For a much fuller account, see Charles Taylor's magisterial *A Secular Age*. If you are looking for a more digestible overview of Taylor's book, see James K. A. Smith, *How (Not) to Be Secular: Reading Charles Taylor* (Grand Rapids: Eerdmans, 2014).

5. Benjamin Storey and Jenna Silber Storey, *Why We Are Restless: On the Modern Quest for Contentment* (Princeton: Princeton University Press, 2021), 33.

6. Sarah Bakewell, *How to Live: Or, A Life of Montaigne in One Question and Twenty Attempts at an Answer* (New York: Other Press, 2010), 139.

7. Michael Allen Gillespie, *The Theological Origins of Modernity* (Chicago: University of Chicago Press, 2008), 199.

8. Michel de Montaigne, *The Complete Works: Essays, Travel Journal, Letters*, trans. Donald Murdoch Frame, Everyman's Library 259 (New York: Knopf, 2003), 9.

9. This famous motto summarizes the argument of Montaigne's essay *Apology for Raymond Sebond*.

Chapter 4: Life in the Attic

1. Mark A. Noll, *The Scandal of the Evangelical Mind*, with new preface and afterword (Grand Rapids: Eerdmans, 2022), 87–90.

2. Alec Ryrie, *Unbelievers: An Emotional History of Doubt* (London: William Collins, 2019), 188–89.

3. For more on how "think like me" can often be trafficked under the admonition "think for yourself," see Alan Jacobs, *How to Think: A Survival Guide for a World at Odds* (New York: Currency, 2017), 31–50.

4. Noll, *Scandal of the Evangelical Mind*, 94–95.

5. For more on a positive Christian vision and its rationale, see Todd Wilson, *Mere Sexuality: Rediscovering the Christian Vision of Sexuality* (Grand Rapids: Zondervan, 2017); and Abigail Favale, *The Genesis of Gender: A Christian Theory* (San Francisco: Ignatius, 2022).

6. Christian Smith, *American Evangelicalism: Embattled and Thriving*, with Michael Emerson, Sally Gallagher, Paul Kennedy, and David Sikkink (Chicago: University of Chicago Press, 1998), 105.

7. James Davison Hunter, *To Change the World: The Irony, Tragedy, and Possibility of Christianity in the Late Modern World* (New York: Oxford University Press, 2010), 218.

8. Hunter, *To Change the World*, 174.

9. See Jonathan T. Pennington, *The Sermon on the Mount and Human Flourishing: A Theological Commentary* (Grand Rapids: Baker Books, 2017).

10. Kevin J. Vanhoozer, *The Drama of Doctrine: A Canonical-Linguistic Approach to Christian Theology* (Louisville: Westminster John Knox, 2005), 291 (emphasis original).

Chapter 5: Finding a Better Posture

1. Charles Taylor, *A Secular Age* (Cambridge, MA: Harvard University Press, 2007), 590, 595.

2. Christopher Hitchens, *God Is Not Great: How Religion Poisons Everything* (New York: Twelve, 2009).

3. John Locke, *A Letter concerning Toleration*, rev. and ed. Mario Montuori (The Hague: Martinus Nijhoff, 1963), as reproduced at The Founders' Constitution, http://press-pubs .uchicago.edu/founders/documents/amendI_assemblys7.html.

4. Charles Taylor, "Afterword: *Apologia pro Libro Suo*," in *Varieties of Secularism in a Secular Age*, ed. Michael Warner, Jonathan VanAntwerpen, and Craig Calhoun (Cambridge, MA: Harvard University Press, 2010), 318.

5. See Jonathan Haidt, *The Righteous Mind: Why Good People Are Divided by Politics and Religion* (New York: Pantheon, 2012), 251.

6. Alasdair MacIntyre, *Whose Justice? Which Rationality?* (Notre Dame, IN: University of Notre Dame Press, 1988).

7. C. S. Lewis, "Meditation in a Toolshed," in *God in the Dock: Essays on Theology and Ethics*, ed. Walter Hooper (Grand Rapids: Eerdmans, 1970), available at https://www.cutsinger.net/wp-content/uploads/2019/08/3_saints_1.pdf.

8. Lewis, "Meditation in a Toolshed."

9. This is what the philosopher John Cottingham describes as the "'humane' turn in philosophy, one that retains the rigour and precision for which the subject is rightly praised, but which aims to embrace all the aspects of our human awareness as we confront the world." John Cottingham, *How to Believe* (New York: Bloomsbury, 2015) x.

Chapter 6: New Atheism

1. Augustine, *Teaching Christianity: De Doctrina Christiana* 2.28, ed. John E. Rotelle, trans. Edmund Hill, The Works of Saint Augustine I/11 (Hyde Park, NY: New City, 2007), 151.

2. Richard Dawkins, *The God Delusion* (Boston: Houghton Mifflin, 2006), 28.

3. Dawkins, *God Delusion*, 28.

4. Richard Dawkins, *The Selfish Gene* (Oxford: Oxford University Press, 1989), 198.

5. Dawkins, *God Delusion*, 24.

6. Dawkins, *God Delusion*, 389.

7. Richard Dawkins, *River Out of Eden: A Darwinian View of Life* (1995; repr., London: Phoenix, 2004), 131–32.

8. Alister E. McGrath, *Dawkins' God: Genes, Memes, and the Meaning of Life* (Malden, MA: Blackwell, 2005), 101–2.

9. Richard Dawkins, "Lions 10, Christians Nil," *Nullafidian* 1, no. 8 (1994), quoted in McGrath, *Dawkins' God*, 89.

10. McGrath, *Dawkins' God*, 89.

11. Baruch A. Shalev, *100 Years of Nobel Prizes* (Los Angeles: Atlantic, 2003), 57.

12. Mary Midgley, *The Solitary Self: Darwin and the Selfish Gene*, Heretics (London: Routledge, 2014), 92–93.

13. C. S. Lewis, *Miracles: A Preliminary Study* (San Francisco: HarperSanFrancisco, 2001), 27–28.

14. Alvin Plantinga, *Where the Conflict Really Lies: Science, Religion, and Naturalism* (Oxford: Oxford University Press, 2011), 316.

15. Martin Luther King Jr., "Remaining Awake through a Great Revolution" (speech, National Cathedral, Washington, DC, March 31, 1968), available at "Remaining Awake Through a Great Revolution (National Cathedral, 3/31/68, Washington D.C.)," January 19, 2015, 46:37, https://youtu.be/okv2QSupAHk.

16. McGrath, *Dawkins' God*, 154.

17. Mary Midgley, *Are You an Illusion?*, Heretics (London: Routledge, 2014), 87.

18. Charles Darwin, *Autobiographies*, ed. Michael Neve and Sharon Messenger, Penguin Classics (New York: Penguin, 2002), 54. Darwin admits that these conclusions were what led him to remain a theist even while writing *On the Origin of Species*. Later in life Darwin described himself as an agnostic on the question of God's existence, particularly due to suffering in the world. See Charles Darwin and Francis Darwin, *The Autobiography of Charles Darwin and Selected Letters* (New York: Dover, 1958), xiii, xx.

19. See Justin L. Barrett, *Born Believers: The Science of Children's Religious Belief* (New York: Atria, 2012).

20. Luc Ferry, *Learning to Live: A User's Manual* (London: Canongate, 2010), 236–37.

21. James Davison Hunter and Paul Nedelisky, *Science and the Good: The Tragic Quest for the Foundations of Morality*, Foundational Questions in Science (New Haven, CT: Yale University Press, 2018), 197.

22. Hunter and Nedelisky, *Science and the Good*, 50–68.

23. Hunter and Nedelisky, *Science and the Good*, 116.

24. Hunter and Nedelisky, *Science and the Good*, 117.

25. McGrath, *Dawkins' God*, 96.

Chapter 7: Optimistic Skepticism

1. Bart D. Ehrman, *Misquoting Jesus: The Story Behind Who Changed the Bible and Why* (New York: HarperOne, 2005), 9–11.

2. Bart D. Ehrman, *God's Problem: How the Bible Fails to Answer Our Most Important Question—Why We Suffer* (New York: HarperOne, 2008), 3.

3. Alvin Plantinga, "Trent Dougherty and Alvin Plantinga: An Interview on Faith and Reason," afterword to *Two Dozen (or So) Arguments for God: The Plantinga Project*, ed. Jerry L. Walls and Trent Dougherty (Oxford: Oxford University Press, 2018), 457.

4. Charles Taylor, *A Secular Age* (Cambridge, MA: Harvard University Press, 2007), 221–25, 260–65.

5. For more on how the multiple perspectives of the Bible work together rather than necessarily against each other, see Richard Bauckham, *Bible and Mission: Christian Witness in a Postmodern World* (Grand Rapids: Baker Books, 2003); Christopher Watkin, *Biblical Critical Theory: How the Bible's Unfolding Story Makes Sense of Life and Culture* (Grand Rapids: Zondervan, 2022), 287–308; Peter Williams, *Can We Trust the Gospels?* (Wheaton: Crossway, 2018), 123–27.

6. Ehrman, *God's Problem*, 189, 195. Most of Ehrman's dissatisfaction with Job seems to stem from the opening and conclusion of the book, rather than the middle sections. He believes there are two authors behind the text of Job, each having contradictory theologies of suffering. According to Ehrman, for the author of the opening and conclusion, suffering is a divine test, but for the writer of the middle sections, there is no divine reason given for suffering. In our view, this is a disjointed and flat reading of a complex literary work with a coherent plotline that the ancient Hebrews understood to be emphasizing multiple non-contradictory responses to suffering. For a more sensitive literary and theological reading of Job, see Bill Kynes and Will Kynes, *Wrestling with Job: Defiant Faith in the Face of Suffering* (Downers Grove, IL: IVP Academic, 2022).

7. Ehrman, *God's Problem*, 15. Again in his conclusion he says that something like this view resonates with him (264–65).

8. These summaries of Ehrman's major points come from Andreas J. Köstenberger, Darrell L. Bock, and Josh D. Chatraw, *Truth in a Culture of Doubt: Engaging Skeptical Challenges to the Bible* (Nashville: B&H, 2014), 20–21.

9. Watkin, *Biblical Critical Theory*, 292.

10. See Stephen John Wykstra, "Rowe's Noseeum Arguments from Evil," in *The Evidential Argument from Evil*, ed. Daniel Howard-Snyder (Bloomington: Indiana University Press, 1996), 139.

11. John Cottingham, *How Can I Believe?* (London: SPCK, 2018), 34.

12. C. S. Lewis, *Mere Christianity* (1943; repr., New York: Macmillan, 1960), 45 (emphasis original).

13. Andrew Delbanco, *The Death of Satan: How Americans Have Lost the Sense of Evil* (New York: Farrar, Straus and Giroux, 1995), 3.

14. Ehrman, *God's Problem*, 276.

15. Ehrman, *God's Problem*, 278 (emphasis original).

16. Francis Spufford, *Unapologetic: Why, Despite Everything, Christianity Can Still Make Surprising Emotional Sense* (San Francisco: HarperOne, 2013), 11.

17. Spufford, *Unapologetic*, 11.

Chapter 8: Open Spirituality

1. For the entire conversation, see "Rhett's Spiritual Deconstruction—One Year Later," Ear Biscuits (YouTube channel), February 21, 2021, video, 1:27:33, https://youtu.be/CnYG6x -aOTk.

2. Charles Taylor, *The Ethics of Authenticity* (Cambridge, MA: Harvard, 1991), 39.

3. Taylor, *Ethics of Authenticity*, 36.

4. Robert Bellah, Richard Madsen, William M. Sullivan, Ann Swidler, and Steven M. Tipton, *Habits of the Heart: Individualism and Commitment in American Life* (Berkeley: University of California Press, 2008), 55–84.

5. Alasdair MacIntyre, *After Virtue: A Study in Moral Theory* (Notre Dame, IN: University of Notre Dame Press, 2007), 16–35.

6. Philip Rieff, *The Triumph of the Therapeutic: Uses of Faith after Freud* (Chicago: University of Chicago Press, 1987), 259–61.

7. Tara Isabella Burton, *Strange Rites: New Religions for a Godless World* (New York: Hachette, 2020), 10 (emphasis original).

8. Kyler Harper, *From Shame to Sin: The Christian Transformation of Sexual Morality in Late Antiquity* (Cambridge, MA: Harvard University Press, 2013), 8.

9. Harper, *From Shame to Sin*, 8.

10. See, e.g., Bridget Phetasy, "I Regret Being a Slut," *Beyond Parody with Bridget Phetasy* (newsletter), Substack, https://bridgetphetasy.substack.com/p/slut-regret.

11. See Christian Smith, "Does Naturalism Warrant a Moral Belief in Universal Benevolence and Human Rights?," in *The Believing Primate: Scientific, Philosophical, and Theological Reflections on the Origin of Religion*, ed. Jeffrey Schloss and Michael Murray (Oxford: Oxford University Press, 2011), 295–98.

12. Christian Smith, *Atheist Overreach* (Oxford: Oxford University Press, 2018), 18. This section is in debt to Smith's work. Though his argument is focused on atheists, at some points we find application for many in this space.

13. "Tom Holland | How Christianity Gained Dominion | A Secular Historian Loses His Faith (In Liberalism)," Speak Life (YouTube channel), October 11, 2020, video, 1:14:13, https://youtu.be/favILmUsVdg.

14. For the entire conversation, see "Seven Types of Atheism with John Gray," *Life after God*, podcast, https://www.spreaker.com/user/lifeaftergod/063-lag-john-gray-final.

Chapter 9: Mythic Truth

1. Tom Holland, *Dominion: How the Christian Revolution Remade the World* (New York: Basic Books, 2019), 540.

2. Ron Dart, "Myth, Memoricide, and Jordan Peterson," in *Myth and Meaning in Jordan Peterson: A Christian Perspective*, ed. Ron Dart (Bellingham, WA: Lexham, 2020), 53.

3. C. G. Jung, *The Archetypes and the Collective Unconscious*, ed. Herbert Read, Michael Fordham, and Gerhard Adler, trans. by R. F. C. Hull (London: Routledge and Kegan Paul, 1959), 43.

4. George Harold Trudeau, "Synthesizing True Myth and Jungian Criticism: Jordan Peterson, Carl Jung, and C. S. Lewis in Conversation," *Heythrop Journal* 62, no. 5 (September 2021): 865, https://doi.org/10.1111/heyj.13984.

5. Jordan B. Peterson, *Maps of Meaning: The Architecture of Belief* (New York: Routledge, 1999), 21.

6. Jordan Peterson, in John Anderson, "Conversations: Featuring Dr. Jordan B Peterson," *Conversations*, podcast, March 27, 2018, comment at 18:06, https://johnanderson.net.au/podcasts/conversations-featuring-dr-jordan-b-peterson-professor-of-psychology-university-of-toronto.

7. Peterson, *Maps of Meaning*, 22.

8. Peterson, *Maps of Meaning*, 21.

9. Peterson, *Maps of Meaning*, 22.

10. See "Political Correctness: A Force for Good? A Munk Debate," Jordan B Peterson (YouTube channel), May 20, 2018, video, 2:04:25 (comments made at 18:05), https://youtu.be/ST6kj9OEYf0.

11. Friedrich Wilhelm Nietzsche, *Beyond Good and Evil: The Philosophy Classic*, Capstone Classics (Hoboken, NJ: Wiley, 2020), 113.

12. Nietzsche, *Beyond Good and Evil*, 114.

13. Nietzsche, *Beyond Good and Evil*, 76.

14. Nietzsche, *Beyond Good and Evil*, 77–78.

15. Kyle Harper, "Christianity and the Roots of Human Dignity in Late Antiquity," in *Christianity and Freedom*, ed. Timothy Samuel Shah and Allen D. Hertzke (Cambridge: Cambridge University Press, 2016), 1:123–48.

16. Jürgen Habermas, *Religion and Rationality: Essays on Reason, God, and Modernity* (Cambridge: Polity, 2002), 149.

17. Trudeau, "Synthesizing True Myth," 868.

18. Tom Holland, "The Power and the Glory," interview by Harry Smart, June 19, 2020, High Profiles, https://highprofiles.info/interview/tom-holland.

19. Jordan B. Peterson, "The Perfect Mode of Being," *Jordan B. Peterson Podcast*, Jordan B Peterson (YouTube channel), March 1, 2021, video, 1:44:19 (comments at 22:18), https://youtu.be/2rAqVmZwqZM.

20. Peterson, "Perfect Mode of Being," 24:00.

21. Peterson, "Perfect Mode of Being," 24:24.

22. Bruce Ashford, "Jordan Peterson and the Chaos of Our Secular Age," in *Myth and Meaning in Jordan Peterson: A Christian Perspective*, ed. Ron Dart (Bellingham, WA: Lexham, 2020), 21–24.

23. Dart, "Myth, Memoricide, and Jordan Peterson," 47.

24. C. S. Lewis, *Christian Reflections* (n.p.: HarperCollins, 2014), 54.

25. C. S. Lewis, "Myth Became Fact," in *God in the Dock*, ed. Walter Hooper (San Francisco: Harper San Francisco, 1994), 58.

26. Holland, "Power and Glory."

27. Augustine, *Confessions* 5.14.24, ed. John E. Rotelle, trans. Maria Boulding, The Works of Saint Augustine I/1 (Hyde Park, NY: New City, 1997), 132.

Interlude

1. See Jason M. Baxter, *The Medieval Mind of C. S. Lewis: How Great Books Shaped a Great Mind* (Downers Grove, IL: IVP, 2022).

2. C. S. Lewis, *The Abolition of Man* (New York: HarperOne, 2001), 79.

3. Baxter, *Medieval Mind*, 164.

4. James Davison Hunter, interview with James K. A. Smith, "The Backdrop of Reality," *Comment*, September 1, 2013, https://comment.org/the-backdrop-of-reality.

5. C. S. Lewis, *The Weight of Glory* (1949; repr., New York: HarperOne, 2001), 31. This section is in debt to Alan Jacobs, *The Narnian: The Life and Imagination of C. S. Lewis* (New York: Harper Collins, 2005), 163–93.

6. Lewis, *Weight of Glory*, 31.

7. Jacobs, *The Narnian*, 173.

8. Baxter, *Medieval Mind*, 165.

9. Mary Midgley, *The Myths We Live By* (New York: Routledge, 2003), 7.

10. Lewis, *Weight of Glory*, 140.

Chapter 10: The Historical Foundation

1. Walker Percy, *Signposts in a Strange Land* (New York: Picador, 1991), 307.

2. See Gary R. Habermas, "The Minimal Facts Approach to the Resurrection of Jesus: The Role of Methodology as a Crucial Component in Establishing Historicity," *Southeastern Theological Review* 3, no. 1 (Summer 2012): 15–26. In this article he also discusses the significance of this approach as used in Michael R. Licona, *The Resurrection of Jesus: A New Historiographical Approach* (Downers Grove, IL: IVP Academic, 2010).

3. For an extensive work on resurrection in the Jewish and non-Jewish worldviews, see N. T. Wright, *The Resurrection of the Son of God*, Christian Origins and the Question of God 3 (Minneapolis: Fortress, 2003).

4. Justin W. Bass, *The Bedrock of Christianity: The Unalterable Facts of Jesus' Death and Resurrection* (Bellingham, WA: Lexham, 2020), 121–22.

5. N. T. Wright, *Who Was Jesus?* (Grand Rapids: Eerdmans, 1993), 63.

6. Richard Bauckham, *Gospel Women: Studies of the Named Women in the Gospels* (Grand Rapids: Eerdmans, 2002), 268–77.

7. While some claims to persecution have been overdramatized, it is nonetheless clear that many of the apostles and early Christians were persecuted for their beliefs. See Eckhard J. Schnabel, *Early Christian Mission* (Downers Grove, IL: InterVarsity, 2004), 2:1533–38.

8. Bart D. Ehrman, *How Jesus Became God: The Exaltation of a Jewish Preacher from Galilee* (New York: HarperOne, 2014), 182–83.

9. Ehrman, *How Jesus Became God*, 186.

10. Ehrman, *How Jesus Became God*, 187.

11. Peter Williams, *Can We Trust the Gospels?* (Wheaton: Crossway, 2018), 134–35.

12. See Matt. 28:11–15. Some see this note as a nonhistorical addition meant to address early critics. For our purposes here, the question of historicity is irrelevant. The fact that Matthew includes it is evidence that early critics claimed the body was stolen.

13. Craig A. Evans, "Getting the Burial Traditions and Evidences Right," in *How God Became Jesus: The Real Origin of Belief in Divine Nature—A Response to Bart D. Ehrman*, ed. Michael F. Bird (Grand Rapids: Zondervan, 2014), 74–75.

14. Jodi Magness, "Jesus' Tomb: What Did It Look Like?," in *Where Christianity Was Born*, ed. Hershel Shanks (Washington, DC: Biblical Archaeology Society, 2006), 224, cited in Evans, "Getting the Burial Traditions and Evidences Right," 77–78.

15. Augustine, *The City of God* 22.5, ed. Boniface Ramsey, trans. William Babcock (Hyde Park, NY: New City, 2013), 501.

16. Augustine, *The City of God* 22.5 (trans. Babcock, 502).

17. Craig S. Keener, *Miracles: The Credibility of the New Testament Accounts*, 2 vols. (Grand Rapids: Baker Academic, 2011).

18. Dale C. Allison Jr., *Encountering Mystery: Religious Experience in a Secular Age* (Grand Rapids: Eerdmans, 2022).

Chapter 11: The Person at the Center

1. Richard Bauckham, *Jesus and the Eyewitnesses: The Gospels as Eyewitness Testimony*, 2nd ed. (Grand Rapids: Eerdmans, 2017), 20.

2. Larry W. Hurtado, *Lord Jesus Christ: Devotion to Jesus in Earliest Christianity* (Grand Rapids: Eerdmans, 2003), 59.

3. Hurtado, *Lord Jesus Christ*, 64.

4. Hurtado, *Lord Jesus Christ*, 7.

5. Hurtado, *Lord Jesus Christ*, 650.

6. Hurtado, *Lord Jesus Christ*, 71.

7. Dane C. Ortlund, *Gentle and Lowly: The Heart of Christ for Sinners and Sufferers* (Wheaton: Crossway, 2020), 17.

8. Jordan Peterson, interview by Joe Rogan, "Joe Rogan Experience #1070 - Jordan Peterson," PowerfulJRE Channel (YouTube channel), January 30, 2018, video, 2:28:52, https://youtu.be/6T7pUEZfgdI.

Chapter 12: The Load-Bearing Walls

1. "Most Christian Countries 2022," World Population Review, https://worldpopulation review.com/country-rankings/most-christian-countries.

2. Andrew F. Walls, *The Missionary Movement in Christian History: Studies in the Transmission of Faith* (Maryknoll, NY: Orbis, 1996), 16–25.

3. Walls, *Missionary Movement*, 3–15.

4. The common phrase "plundering the Egyptians" serves as shorthand for Augustine's argument on adopting truth wherever it may be found. Just as the Israelites, under the direction of God, took Egyptian gold when fleeing their captivity and put it to good use, Christians today can take truth that is found even in secular places and put it to good use. See Augustine, *Teaching Christianity: De Doctrina Christiana*, ed. John E. Rotelle, trans. Edmund Hill, The Works of Saint Augustine I/11 (Hyde Park, NY: New City, 2007), 170.

5. See Matthew Lee Anderson, "Will the Controversies 'Fade Away'?," Respectful Conversation, January 3, 2016, http://www.respectfulconversation.net/hs-conversation/2016

/1/3/will-the-controversies-fade-away.html; cf. Trevin Wax, "Is Marriage an 'Architectural Doctrine' of the Christian Faith?," The Gospel Coalition, February 29, 2016, https://www.thegospelcoalition.org/blogs/trevin-wax/is-marriage-an-architectural-doctrine-of-the-christian-faith.

6. Michael Bird, *What Christians Ought to Believe: An Introduction to Christian Doctrine through the Apostles' Creed* (Grand Rapids: Zondervan, 2016), 32.

7. Bird, *What Christians Ought to Believe*, 32–33.

8. For the sake of space, we are limiting our focus to the Apostles' Creed, even though the Nicene Creed is critical in securing the essential truths about the person of Christ.

9. Ben Myers, *Apostles' Creed: A Guide to the Ancient Catechism* (Bellingham, WA: Lexham, 2018), 2.

10. The Apostles' Creed, available at Anglicans Online, http://www.anglicansonline.org/basics/apostles.html.

11. Augustine, "Sermon 215," in *Sermons (184—229Z) on the Liturgical Seasons*, ed. John E. Rotelle, trans. Edmund Hill, The Works of Saint Augustine III/6 (Hyde Park, NY: New City, 1993).

12. Augustine, *The Literal Meaning of Genesis* 19, 39 (Hyde Park, NY: New City, 2002), 186.

13. Augustine, *Literal Meaning of Genesis* 19, 39 (pp. 186–87).

14. See David Hutchings and James C. Ungureanu, *Of Popes and Unicorns: Science, Christianity, and How the Conflict Thesis Fooled the World* (New York: Oxford University, 2022), which undermines, from a historical perspective, the alleged necessary conflict between Christianity and science. Also see Jeff Hardin, Ronald L. Numbers, and Ronald A. Binzley, eds., *The Warfare between Science and Religion: The Idea That Wouldn't Die* (Baltimore: John Hopkins University, 2018). For a work that questions this conflict by way of "facts on the ground" empirical studies, see Elaine Howard Ecklund and Christopher P. Scheitle, *Religion vs. Science: What Religious People Really Think* (New York: Oxford University, 2017).

15. Augustine, *Literal Meaning of Genesis* 18, 37 (pp. 185–86).

16. For more on Augustine and the doctrine of creation, see Gavin Ortlund, *Retrieving Augustine's Doctrine of Creation: Ancient Wisdom for Current Controversy* (Downers Grove, IL: InterVarsity, 2020); Alister McGrath, *A Fine-Tuned Universe: The Quest for God in Science and Theology* (Louisville: Westminster John Knox, 2009), 95–108. For recent proposals directly taking both Gen. 1–3 and mainstream science seriously, see Joshua Swamidass, *The Genealogical Adam and Eve: The Surprising Science of Universal Ancestry* (Downers Grove, IL: IVP, 2021); C. John Collins, *Reading Genesis Well: Navigating History, Poetry, Science, and Truth in Genesis 1–11* (Grand Rapids: Zondervan, 2018); Matthew Levering, *Engaging the Doctrine of Creation: Cosmos, Creatures, and the Wise and Good Creator* (Grand Rapids: Baker Academic, 2017); Timothy Keller, "Creation, Evolution, and the Christian Lay Person," BioLogos, February 23, 2012, https://biologos.org/articles/creation-evolution-and-christian-laypeople.

17. C. S. Lewis, *The Great Divorce* (San Francisco: HarperOne, 2001), 312–29; and N. T. Wright, *Surprised by Hope: Rethinking Heaven, the Resurrection, and the Mission of the Church* (New York: HarperOne, 2008), 175–86.

18. Christopher Watkin, *Biblical Critical Theory: How the Bible's Unfolding Story Makes Sense of Life and Culture* (Grand Rapids: Zondervan, 2022), 184.

19. C. S. Lewis, "God in the Dock," in *Essay Collection: Faith, Christianity, and the Church*, ed. Lesley Walmsey (London: HarperCollins, 2000), 36.

20. Fyodor Dostoyevsky, *The Brothers Karamazov*, trans. Constance Garnett (New York: Macmillan, 1922), 219.

21. Augustine, *Sermons*, ed. John E. Rotelle, trans. Edmund Hill, The Works of Saint Augustine III/11 (Hyde Park, NY: New City, 1997), 207–9. Pastor Timothy Keller mirrors a similar posture, admitting that we can't provide a certain answer to this question. But by providing hypothetical explanations—e.g., the appeal to "middle knowledge" that bases God's salvific work on whether an unreached person would have accepted the gospel if they had heard—we can be confident that God has a more true, full, and good way to handle this question than we can imagine ourselves. See "'Making Sense of God,' with Tim Keller," *Mere Fidelity* (podcast), 54:05 (comments span 43:30–53:30), December 13,

2016, https://merefidelity.com/podcast/making-sense-of-god-with-tim-keller. For a review of Christian positions on this issue, see Daniel Strange, *The Possibility of Salvation among the Unevangelized: An Analysis of Inclusivism in Recent Evangelical Theology* (Eugene, OR: Wipf & Stock, 2007).

22. J. R. R. Tolkien, *The Lord of the Rings* (New York: William Morrow, 2012), 951.

Chapter 13: Wagering Wisely

1. Peter Kreeft, *Christianity for Modern Pagans: Pascal's Pensées* (Ignatius: San Francisco, 1993), 9 (emphasis original).

2. Benjamin Storey and Jenna Silber Storey, *Why We Are Restless: On the Modern Quest for Contentment* (Princeton: Princeton University Press, 2021), 92.

3. Jonathan Haidt, *The Happiness Hypothesis: Finding Modern Truth in Ancient Wisdom* (New York: Basic Books, 2006), 13.

4. Iain McGilchrist, *The Master and His Emissary: The Divided Brain and the Making of the Western World*, new expanded ed. (New Haven, CT: Yale University Press, 2019), 185.

5. Iain McGilchrist, *The Matter with Things: Our Brains, Our Delusions and the Unmaking of the World* (London: Perspectiva, 2021), loc. 30636 of 50425, Kindle.

6. Storey and Storey, *Why We Are Restless*, 65–66, quoting Pascal's *Pensées*.

7. David Brooks, *The Second Mountain: The Quest for a Moral Life* (New York: Random House, 2019), xx.

8. Brooks, *Second Mountain*, xxii.

9. Brooks, *Second Mountain*, 31–37.

10. This illustration has been modified from how I (Josh) used it in Joshua D. Chatraw and Mark D. Allen, *The Augustine Way: Retrieving a Vision for the Church's Apologetic Witness* (Grand Rapids: Baker Academic, 2023).

11. Augustine, *Confessions* 6.9, trans. Sarah Ruden (New York: Modern Library, 2017), 146.

12. Storey and Storey, *Why We Are Restless*, 87.

13. Blaise Pascal, *Pensées*, trans. A. J. Krailsheimer (New York: Penguin, 1995), 124.

14. Graeme Hunter, *Pascal the Philosopher: An Introduction* (Toronto: University of Toronto Press, 2013), 26.

Chapter 14: A Window to See Through

1. Peter Kreeft, *Christianity for Modern Pagans: Pascal's Pensées* (San Francisco: Ignatius, 1993), 47.

2. See N. T. Wright, *History and Eschatology: Jesus and the Promise of Natural Theology* (Waco: Baylor University Press, 2019); N. T. Wright, *Broken Signposts: How Christianity Makes Sense of the World* (New York: HarperOne, 2020).

3. See Jonathan Haidt, *The Righteous Mind: Why Good People Are Divided by Politics and Religion* (New York: Pantheon, 2012), 234–40.

4. Haidt, *Righteous Mind*, 52–58.

5. Thomas Hobbes, *Leviathan* (Minneapolis: Lerner, 2018), 9.

6. Christopher Watkin, *Biblical Critical Theory: How the Bible's Unfolding Story Makes Sense of Life and Culture* (Grand Rapids: Zondervan, 2022), 64.

7. For further reading on competing theories surrounding human value, see Nicholas Wolterstorff, *Justice: Rights and Wrongs* (Princeton: Princeton University Press, 2008).

8. Fyodor Dostoevsky, *The Brothers Karamazov*, trans. Constance Garnett (New York: Macmillan, 1922), 241–42.

9. Cameron J. Anderson, *The Faithful Artist: A Vision for Evangelicalism and the Arts*, Studies in Theology and the Arts (Downers Grove, IL: IVP Academic, 2016), 213.

10. Wright, *History and Eschatology*, 227.

11. Bart Ehrman, *God's Problem: How the Bible Fails to Answer Our Most Important Question—Why We Suffer* (New York: HarperOne, 2008), 278.

12. Marilynne Robinson, *What Are We Doing Here? Essays* (New York: Picador, 2019), 110–13.

13. J. R. R. Tolkien, *The Return of the King,* vol. 3 of *The Lord of the Rings* (New York: William Morrow, 2012), 95.

14. Augustine, "Sermon 198," in *Sermons (Newly Discovered),* ed. John E. Rotelle, trans. Edmund Hill, The Works of Saint Augustine III/11 (Hyde Park, NY: New City, 1997), 180.

15. Charles Taylor, *A Secular Age* (Cambridge, MA: Harvard University Press, 2007), 711.

16. Bertrand Russell, "A Free Man's Worship," in *The Basic Writings of Bertrand Russell,* ed. R. E. Egner and L. E. Denonn (London: Routledge, 1992), 67.

17. Taylor, *Secular Age,* 718.

Chapter 15: "But I Still Can't Believe! Now What?"

1. Blaise Pascal, *Pensées,* trans. A. J. Krailsheimer (New York: Penguin, 1995), 124–25.

2. See Charles Taylor, *Modern Social Imaginaries* (Durham, NC: Duke University Press, 2003), 23; Charles Taylor, *A Secular Age* (Cambridge, MA: Harvard University Press, 2007), 325, 549. For more on how scholars describe human perception of "rationality," see Alister McGrath, *The Territories of Human Reason: Science and Theology in an Age of Multiple Rationalities* (Oxford: Oxford University Press, 2019), 25.

3. Richard Beck, *Hunting Magic Eels: Recovering an Enchanted Faith in a Skeptical Age* (Minneapolis: Broadleaf, 2021), 5, citing Andrew Root, *The Pastor in a Secular Age: Ministry to People Who No Longer Need a God* (Grand Rapids: Baker Academic, 2019), 270.

4. Beck, *Hunting Magic Eels,* 5.

5. Beck, *Hunting Magic Eels,* 70.

6. Pascal himself does provide various reasons to respect and believe in Christianity. Two of his favorites are the fit between Christianity and human nature and the fulfillment of biblical prophecy.

7. Iain McGilchrist, *The Matter with Things: Our Brains, Our Delusions and the Unmaking of the World* (London: Perspectiva, 2021), loc. 29488 of 50425, Kindle.

8. James K. A. Smith, *Desiring the Kingdom: Worship, Worldview, and Cultural Formation,* Cultural Liturgies 1 (Grand Rapids: Baker Academic, 2009).

9. Though he uses it differently, the idea of an alien anthropologist of religion comes from Andrew F. Walls, *The Missionary Movement in Christian History: Studies in the Transmission of Faith* (Maryknoll, NY: Orbis, 1996), 3.

10. For more support, see Tara Isabella Burton, *Strange Rites: New Religions for a Godless World* (New York: Hachette, 2020).

11. Pascal, *Pensées,* quoted by Benjamin Storey and Jenna Silber Storey, *Why We Are Restless: On the Modern Quest for Contentment* (Princeton: Princeton University Press, 2021), 74.

12. Storey and Storey, *Why We Are Restlesss,* 76.

13. "The Persuaders," directed by Barak Goodman and Rachel Dretzin, *Frontline,* season 2004, episode 15, aired November 9, 2004, https://www.pbs.org/video/frontline-persuaders, transcript available at www.pbs.org/wgbh/pages/frontline/shows/persuaders/etc/script.html.

14. Eugene H. Peterson, *A Long Obedience in the Same Direction: Discipleship in an Instant Society,* 20th anniv. ed. (Downers Grove, IL: InterVarsity, 2000).

15. Pascal, *Pensées,* 285.

Chapter 16: Practicing Your Way through Doubt

1. Alan Jacobs, *The Narnian: The Life and Imagination of C. S. Lewis* (New York: Harper Collins, 2005), 293.

2. Richard Beck, *Hunting Magic Eels: Recovering an Enchanted Faith in a Skeptical Age* (Minneapolis: Broadleaf, 2021), 15.

3. C. S. Lewis, *Letters to Malcom: Chiefly on Prayer* (London: William Collins, 2000), 101.

4. Timothy P. O'Malley, *Invitation and Encounter: Evangelizing through the Sacraments* (Huntington, IN: Our Sunday Visitor, 2022), 14.

5. Charles Taylor, *A Secular Age* (Cambridge, MA: Harvard University Press, 2007), 727.

6. Taylor, *A Secular Age*, 720.

7. Taylor, *A Secular Age*, 723.

8. Timothy M. Gallagher, *The Examen Prayer: Ignatian Wisdom for Our Lives Today* (New York: Crossroad, 2006), 43–44.

9. Jan Johnson, *Meeting God in Scripture: A Hands-On Guide to Lectio Divina* (Downers Grove, IL: IVP Books, 2016), 13.

10. C. S. Lewis, *The Screwtape Letters* (New York: HarperOne, 1996), 64.

11. Augustine, *Confessions* 4.12.18, ed. John E. Rotelle, trans. Maria Boulding, The Works of Saint Augustine I/1 (Hyde Park, NY: New City, 1997), 103.

12. Sarah Coakley, interview by Robert Lawrence Kuhn, *Closer to Truth*, episode 1103, "Why Believe in God?," aired July 14, 2015, https://www.closertotruth.com/episodes/why-believe-god. Thanks to Justin Ariel Bailey (*Reimagining Apologetics: The Beauty of Faith in a Secular Age* [Downers Grove, IL: IVP Academic, 2020], 242–46) for making us aware of this video.

Epilogue

1. Douglas Kaine McKelvey, *Every Moment Holy*, vol. 1 (Nashville: Rabbit Room, 2019); McKelvey, *Every Moment Holy*, vol. 2, *Death, Grief, and Hope* (Nashville: Rabbit Room, 2021).

2. McKelvey, *Every Moment Holy*, 1:164. Used with permission.

3. McKelvey, *Every Moment Holy*, 1:166. Used with permission.

4. McKelvey, *Every Moment Holy*, 1:167. Used with permission.